WHO'S WHO OF HORRORS

WHO'S WHO OF HORRORS

An A to Z of **loathsome lives**

By Tracey Turner

A division of Hodder Headline Limited

© Tracey Turner 2005
Published in Great Britain in 2005
by Hodder Children's Books
Design by Andrew Summers, Planet Creative
Cover design: Hodder Children's Books

10 9 8 7 6 5 4 3 2 1

A catalogue record for this book is available from the British Library

ISBN:0340902949

Printed by Bookmarque Ltd, Croydon, Surrey

The paper and board used in this paperback by Hodder Children's
Books are natural recyclable products made from wood grown in
sustainable forests.
The manufacturing processes conform to the environmental
regulations of the country of origin.

Hodder Children's Books
a division of Hodder Headline Limited
338 Euston Road
London NW1 3BH

WHO'S WHO OF HORRORS

Who *is* Who?

A *Who's Who* is a book that lists extremely posh or famous people. Many of the people in this *Who's Who* are famous and some of them are extremely posh. But the reason they're included here is because they have one thing in common:

they're horrors.

Being a horror can mean a variety of different things:

- torturing, murdering, or a bit of both
- producing something disgusting
- dying in a particularly unpleasant manner
- having a revolting habit.

As you will discover, there are many ways that the above list can be put into practice.

In these pages you'll meet 150 characters you definitely wouldn't want to meet in real life, including The Cross-eyed Lambeth Poisoner, The Teenage Butcher, Juana the Mad and Ismail the Bloodthirsty. They've been gathered here from the Wild West, Ancient Rome, Medieval Italy and Victorian Britain, into a handy A-Z format. Each individual has his or her Horrible Deeds documented, along with other relevant details such as Occupation, Horrible End and Specialist Skills. Where a person's name appears in *italics*, it means you can find out more by looking up their own separate entry.

Read on and shudder...

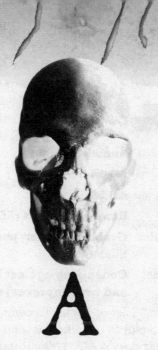

A

George Abbot

Nationality:	**English**
Born:	**1562**
Died:	**1633**
Occupation:	**Archbishop of Canterbury**

Horrible Deeds: Imposing extremely harsh punishments.

While he was teaching at Balliol College, Oxford, George Abbot sent 140 of his students to prison for not taking their hats off in his presence. He disapproved of a preacher called Alexander Leighton, so he had him tied to a stake and flogged before being put in the pillory, branded on the face, his nose split and his ears cut off. He had other so-called heretics (people who go against the teachings of the Church) suspended from chains.

A

Agrippina

Nationality:	**Ancient Roman**
Born:	**AD 15**
Died:	**AD 59**
Occupation:	**Roman Empress (AD 49-54).**
Specialist Skills:	**Grabbing power; poisoning husbands.**
Horrible Deeds:	**Conspiring against her brother and two (unproven) murders.**

Agrippina was the sister of Roman Emperor *Caligula*. She was involved in a plot to get rid of him and was forced into exile until Caligula died in AD 41. She is supposed to have killed her second husband, Saullustius Passienus Crispus, probably with poison, to get at his money. She then married husband number three, the Emperor *Claudius*, despite the fact that he was her uncle. It's likely that Agrippina gave Claudius poisoned mushrooms, which killed him in AD 54. But before she got rid of him she made sure that Claudius had adopted her son from her first marriage, *Nero*, so that Nero would be the next Roman Emperor instead of Claudius's own son.

Horrible End: Agrippina was finally murdered herself in AD 59 by her son, the Emperor Nero.

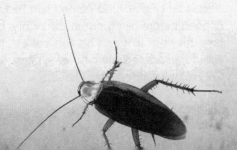

Alexander III

Aka:	**Alexander the Great, Alexander the Conqueror**
Nationality:	**Macedonian**
Born:	**356 BC**
Died:	**323 BC**
Occupation:	**King of Macedonia (336-323 BC)**
Specialist Skills:	**Conquering; being ruthless**

Horrible Deeds: Various, during the course of his conquest of most of the known world.

When he became king at the age of 20, Alexander's first act was to execute anyone who might have some claim to his throne, then he set off to expand his empire. When he conquered the Persian capital of Persepolis, he looted the city and set fire to the famously beautiful Palace of Xerxes. After he stormed the city of Tyre, he executed thousands of the city's survivors (it's said he had 2,000 crucified), and he sold many thousands more into slavery. Alexander made sure that the captured Persian king, Bessus, suffered by having his ears and nose cut off before being publicly executed.

Alexander also executed several of his friends. Philotas was accused of failing to tell Alexander about a plot – he was almost certainly innocent, but Alexander had him tortured on the rack and then executed. He also had Philotas's father, an old general called Parmenion, stabbed to death. Clitus the Black had saved Alexander's life in battle, but Alexander murdered him by running him through with a lance during a drunken argument.

Horrible End: Alexander died of a mysterious illness aged

A

33 after a prolonged bout of drinking – he might have been poisoned by one of his enemies, or even his wife. According to legend, Alexander's body was embalmed in a container of honey and buried in a glass coffin.

Hypatia of Alexandria

Nationality:	Egyptian
Born:	About AD 370
Died:	AD 415
Occupation:	Mathematician, astronomer and philosopher

Horrible Deed: Hypatia was a pagan who was blamed for the trouble in Egypt between the Roman ruler of Egypt, Orestes, and the Christian leader, Cyril, and met with a horrible end.

Horrible End: A mob of fanatical Christians murdered Hypatia by skinning her, chopping her body into pieces then burning it. Some said Cyril was responsible.

Ashurbanipal

Nationality:	Assyrian
Born:	?
Died:	about 631
Occupation:	King of Assyrian Empire (668-627 BC)
Specialist Skills:	Conquering; librarianship (he assembled the first proper library in the world)

Horrible Deeds: Ruthlessly punishing his enemies.

Ashurbanipal boasted that he had fed dead Babylonian leaders to dogs, pigs, wolves and eagles. In a huge triumphal procession to celebrate his victories, he harnessed three Elamite princes and an Arabian king to his chariot. He forced an Arab leader to live as a watchdog, chained up with collar round his neck, at Ashburnipal's city gates. He is also supposed to have had another enemy leader pickled alive in a barrel of salt.

Attila the Hun

Aka:	**Scourge of God**
Nationality:	**Hun (the Huns were nomads who roamed the steppes of Asia)**
Born:	**About AD 403**
Died:	**AD 453**
Occupation:	**King of the Huns (434-453)**
Specialist Skills:	**Conquering, plundering and pillaging.**

Horrible Deeds: Leading the Hun tribes in a deadly rampage across much of Europe and Asia, and killing his brother.

Attila invaded the Eastern Roman Empire, Germany, Gaul and Italy, killing people, laying waste to cities and leaving a trail of destruction wherever he went. Defeated tribes were forced to pay huge taxes to the Huns. Attila ruled jointly with his elder brother Bleda until 445, when Attila murdered him. His favourite hobby was hunting: when he'd captured an animal, he liked to disembowel it.

Horrible End: Attila died on his last ever wedding night (he is supposed to have had 300 wives) when he got drunk, had a nosebleed and choked on the blood. After he'd been buried, the Huns executed the people who buried him and his treasures, so that his grave would never be discovered.

Quiz

Which conqueror died of a nosebleed?

a) Attila the Hun
b) Alexander the Great
c) Genghis Khan

Aurangzeb

Aka:	**Aurangzeb the Intolerant**
Nationality:	**Indian**
Born:	**1618**
Died:	**1707**
Occupation:	**Emperor of India (1658-1707)**

Horrible Deeds: Imprisoning his father, killing his brothers and exiling his son, destroying Hindu temples and executing non-Muslims.

In his struggle to become the next emperor of India, Aurangzeb imprisoned his father at Agra Fort and defeated his brother and rightful heir to the throne, Dara Shikoh, who died in battle. Then Aurangzeb ordered the execution of his two other brothers.

Once in power, Aurangzeb wanted the country to be strictly Muslim, so he destroyed Hindu temples and imposed a tax on non-Muslims. There was a revolt against the tax, which was supported by Aurangzeb's son Akbar. Aurangzeb personally led the troops that defeated the rebels and drove his son into exile. A chief who had helped Akbar was tortured and murdered on Aurangzeb's orders. When the Sikh leader Tegh Bahadur refused to become a Muslim, Aurangzeb had him executed. He also killed four sons of Tegh Bahadur's successor.

Answer: a

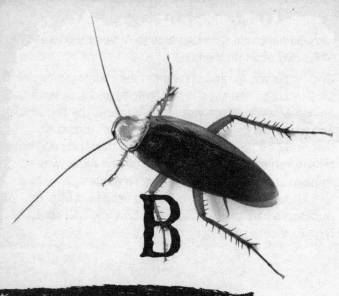

Reverend Thomas Baker

Nationality: English

Born: 1832

Died: 1867

Occupation: Missionary

Horrible Deed: see Horrible End

Horrible End: The Reverend Thomas Baker was trying to spread Christianity in the remote Fijian village of Navatusila of Navosa on the island of Viti Levu. Not realizing that it was against the law to touch the head of a chief, Baker made the fatal mistake of removing a comb from the chief's head. Baker and eight of his followers were immediately clubbed to death, cooked and eaten by the Fijians. Many years later, in 2003, the villagers of Navatusila of Navosa made an elaborate apology to ten of the Reverend Baker's descendants, presenting them with woven mats, whales' teeth and a slaughtered cow in a ceremony attended by the Prime Minister of Fiji.

Graham Barker

Nationality: **Australian**
Born: **1965**
Horrible Deed: Collecting his own navel fluff for over 20 years.

Graham has his own website which documents his unusual collection, and has a place in the Guinness Book of Records for it.

Elizabeth Bathory

Aka: **The Blood Countess**
Nationality: **Transylvanian**
Born: **1560**
Died: **1614**
Occupation: **Countess**
Horrible Deeds: Torturing and murdering people, especially young women.

Countess Bathory had always been cruel, beating her servants if they failed to please her. Over time, alone in the remote Castle Csejthe, she set up her own dungeon and tortured unfortunate victims who had been lured to the castle with the promise of work.

As she got older, Countess Bathory had the idea that

B

bathing in the blood of young women would make her skin more youthful. So she began ordering her helpers to find young girls, who were then killed and drained of their blood – often they were tortured first. In 1610 her castle was raided on the orders of the Emperor of Transylvannia and her dreadful deeds were uncovered. She is thought to have killed hundreds of young women.

Horrible End: Elizabeth Bathory's punishment was to be walled up in her own castle. She was sealed into her bedroom, with a small opening for food, and remained imprisoned there until she died four years later. Her accomplices at the castle had their fingers torn off before being burned alive.

Quiz

Hannah Beswick was afraid of being buried alive and asked her doctor to keep her body and check on it every year. Where did he keep the body?

a) Under his bed.
b) In a grandfather clock.
c) In a chair in the dining room.

Sawney Bean

Nationality: Scottish
Born: About 1400
Died: ?
Occupation: Cave-dwelling mass-murderer and cannibal.

Horrible Deeds: Killing and eating passers-by.

Sawney Bean and his extended family of children and grandchildren (48 altogether) lived in a cave on the Galloway coast. They lived by robbing people, then killing and eating them. When the Beans were finally discovered they were thought to have murdered and eaten hundreds of people.

The horrible story of Sawney Bean and his family's unusual diet was first reported a hundred years after it took place – some suggest that it was a story invented by the English who wanted to give the Scots a bad name.

Horrible End: When they were discovered the Bean family members were immediately taken by soldiers and executed without trial.

Hannah Beswick

Nationality: English
Born: 1680
Died: 1758
Occupation: Bonkers old lady.

Answer: b

Horrible Deed: Not being buried until 110 years after her death.

Horrible End: Hannah was terrified of being buried alive, so she left £25,000 in her will to her doctor, Charles White, on the condition that her body should not be buried and that he should visit her regularly after her death. The doctor had Hannah embalmed and kept her in a grandfather clock in his home. He visited her once a year on the anniversary of her death, as he had promised.

After Dr White died, Hannah ended up at the Manchester Musem of Natural History. When the museum moved to a new building in 1868, Hannah's body was examined and finally buried.

William H Bonney Junior

Aka:	**Billy the Kid**
Nationality:	**American**
Born:	**1859 or 1860**
Died:	**1881**
Occupation:	**Outlaw**

Horrible Deeds: Murdering at least 27 people.

Billy the Kid killed his first victim when he was just fourteen, by stabbing him to death. He went on a killing spree in revenge for the murder of a friend, and became a wanted man after he killed a sheriff, his seventeenth victim. He is supposed to have murdered at least 27 men before he was killed at the age of 21 or 22. He was tried for murder and sentenced to hang, but escaped from jail – killing two deputies on his way out.

Horrible End: Billy the Kid was finally tracked down by Sheriff Pat Garrett, who shot him dead.

Lizzie Borden

Nationality:	**American**
Born:	**1860**
Died:	**1927**

Horrible Deeds: Murdering her parents (probably).

Lizzie was put on trial for the brutal murders of Mr and Mrs Borden, her father and stepmother, in Massachusetts in 1892, but she was acquitted. However, evidence suggests that she was very likely the killer. Mrs Borden was killed with an axe – she was struck eighteen times. A few hours later, Mr Borden was struck eleven times with the same axe, his head nearly hacked in two. Despite her acquittal, Lizzie was immortalised in the rhyme:

Lizzie Borden bought an axe
Gave her mother forty whacks
When she saw what she had done
She gave her father forty-one.

Cesare Borgia

Aka:	**Duke Valentino**
Nationality:	**Italian**
Born:	**About 1475**
Died:	**1507**
Occupation:	**Cardinal and commander of the Pope's army.**

B

Horrible Deeds: Murdering people, including his brother-in-law and (possibly) his own brother.

Cesare was made a cardinal at the age of 19 by his father *Rodrigo Borgia*, who was Pope Alexander VI. His elder brother, Juan, had been made commander of the Pope's army. When Juan died in 1497 Cesare took his job, and many people suspected Cesare of killing Juan himself. Cesare's sister Lucretia had a Spanish boyfriend called Pedro Calderon and Cesare was probably responsible for having him killed and his body thrown into the River Tiber. In 1500 Cesare also murdered his brother-in-law, Alfonso – he had been attacked by assassins but was making a good recovery when Cesare stepped in to finish the job. Two of his own army commanders turned against him in 1502 (one of whom was *Oliverotto da Fermo*): he pretended to reconcile with them and invited them to a meeting, where he had them killed.

Quiz

Which American woman was cleared of murdering her parents with an axe, but was remembered as their killer in a rhyme?

a) Lizzie Borden
b) Mary Ann Cotton
c) Pocahontas

Rodrigo Borgia

Aka:	**Pope Alexander VI**
Nationality:	**Spanish**
Born:	**1431**
Died:	**1503**
Occupation:	**Pope (1492-1503)**
Specialist Skills:	**Getting rich.**

Horrible Deeds: Having people murdered and accepting bribes.

Rodrigo Borgia became Pope in 1492 and made it obvious straight away that he intended to use his position to make himself and his family as powerful and rich as possible. He sold off positions of power, and accused wealthy people of made-up offences so that he could confiscate their property after they were imprisoned or executed. Anyone who spoke out against him could be punished with death.

Horrible End: It's thought that Rodrigo drank a glass of poisoned wine he had intended for one of his guests. The coffin that had been made for him wasn't big enough, so Rodrigo's body had to be stuffed into it as best it could and covered over with an oilcloth.

Marlon Brando

Nationality:	**American**
Born:	**1924**
Died:	**2004**
Occupation:	**Actor**

Horrible Deed: Biting a frog.

Answer: a

21

B

Marlon Brando became famous as a great actor and, in later years, as a great eater. He would sometimes eat two whole chickens for dinner, and often gorged himself on hamburgers and hotdogs. On a film set one day he suddenly grabbed a live frog from a stream and took a bite out of the creature before throwing it back.

Frank Buckland

Nationality:	**English**
Born:	**1826**
Died:	**1888**
Occupation:	**Naturalist and eccentric**
Specialist Skills:	**Hearty appetite.**

Horrible Deeds: Eating a variety of unusual animals.

Frank Buckland was known as an eccentric and kept a variety of strange pets at his home, including monkeys, a jaguar and a jackass. But his eating habits were even more unusual. Buckland's menu included squirrel pie, mice cooked in batter, hedgehogs, crocodile, a panther that had been buried in the Surrey Zoological gardens (he had the animal dug up and roasted), elephant's trunk soup, kangaroo, giraffe (killed in a zoo fire) and rhinoceros pie. Frank's father, William Buckland, also liked to eat unusual food – the strangest thing he ever ate was the mummified heart of King Louis XIV.

William Burke

Nationality: Irish

Born: 1792

Died: 1829

Occupation: **General labourer and murderer**

Horrible Deeds: Body-snatching and murdering.

William Burke was working as a labourer in Edinburgh when an old man in his lodging house died owing him money. The man who owned the lodging house, *William Hare*, had the idea of selling the body to a surgeon called Dr Robert Knox, who needed corpses for dissection. They were well paid for the body and got back more than the money Burke was owed. The pair then began digging up corpses that had recently been buried and selling them to Knox and other doctors. They soon found that the demand from the doctors was higher than they could keep up with, so Burke and Hare began murdering people to keep up the supply of bodies. They would lure people back to their lodging house, get them drunk and then suffocate them, with the help of their girlfriends, Helen McDougal and Maggie Laird.

Burke and Hare were discovered when they carelessly left a body in the lodging house where other people could see it. By this time the pair had killed at least fifteen people. William Hare and Maggie Laird gave evidence against the others and so were allowed to go free, but William Burke and Helen McDougal were tried, and Burke was found guilty.

Horrible End: William Burke was hanged in 1829.

C

Julius Caesar

Aka:	**Gaius Julius Caesar**
Nationality:	**Ancient Roman**
Born:	**About 100 BC**
Died:	**44 BC**
Occupation:	**Lawyer, general and dictator of the Roman Republic**
Specialist Skills:	**Conquering.**

Horrible Deeds: Enslaving and torturing barbarian tribes.

Julius Caesar was a successful general, defeating many of the European tribes and putting them under Roman rule. He could be cruel, particularly with tribes who rebelled. In 56 he had the whole of the rebellious Veneti tribe sold into slavery once he'd defeated them. The surviving members of the Bellovaci rebels all had their hands cut off by Caesar.

C

When he was a young man, Caesar was captured by pirates who held him to ransom. He became friendly with his captors but warned them that he'd have his revenge. Caesar managed to raise the money for his ransom and the pirates set him free. Then he found and captured the pirates and had them all crucified.

Horrible End: Caesar was on his way to a meeting when he was surrounded by a group of politicians who'd been conspiring against him. They pulled daggers from underneath their togas and stabbed Caesar to death. He received twenty-three stab wounds.

Quiz

Which famous actor bit a frog on a film set?

a) Tom Cruise
b) Marlon Brando
c) Clint Eastwood

Adam of Caithness

Nationality:	**Scottish**
Born:	**?**
Died:	**1222**
Occupation:	**Bishop of Caithness**

C

Horrible Deeds: Demanding huge taxes and throwing out of the Church anyone who couldn't pay.

Horrible End: An angry crowd attacked the Bishop on 13 September 1222 and burned him to death in his own kitchen – some reports say he was boiled in butter. The crowd's punishment by Scottish King Alexander II was even worse: the leaders were hanged, while the rest (about 80 people) had their hands and feet cut off.

Caligula

Aka:	**Gaius Caesar Germanicus**
Nationality:	**Ancient Roman**
Born:	**AD 12**
Died:	**AD 41**
Occupation:	**Emperor of Rome (AD 37-41).**
Specialist Skills:	**Devising horrible methods of execution; being mad.**

Horrible Deeds: Many different acts of bonkers cruelty.

Caligula became emperor in AD 37. Many people suspected that he or the army commander Macro had murdered the previous emperor, Tiberius. One of his first acts as emperor was to kill his cousin, Gemellus, who was supposed to rule jointly with Caligula. Not long afterwards he also executed Macro, his supporter and possibly the murderer of Tiberius.

When his sister Drusilla died in 38, Caligula made laughing in public or in private an offence punishable by death. He began a series of murders, many of them particularly cruel: he forced parents to witness the execution of their children and sometimes made them dine with him afterwards. One senator protested his innocence when he was thrown to the lions – Caligula had him rescued, then had his tongue cut out before he was thrown back. He cut off the arms and legs of another senator and had them piled up in front of him, before doing same with the man's insides.

Caligula had an extravagant lifestyle and needed money to pay for it, so he had rich people murdered and took their land and property. Caligula declared himself to be a god and demanded worship, and anyone who upset him faced torture and death: he had people beaten with chains and burned to death. Some reports say that he condemned prisoners to death so that there was a plentiful supply of victims for the wild animals in the bloodthirsty games.

Horrible End: Eventually Caligula was assassinated by group of politicians. They stabbed him to death after he'd been to the games in AD 41. His wife, Caesonia, and daughter were also murdered.

Al Capone

Aka:	**Scarface**
Nationality:	**Italian-American**
Born:	**1899**
Died:	**1947**
Occupation:	**Gangster**
Specialist Skills:	**Frightening people.**

Horrible Deeds: Various gangland killings.

Al Capone was a gangster who made most of his huge wealth by supplying alcohol, which was banned in 1920s America. He became the most important criminal in 1920s

Chicago and was known as "Public Enemy Number One" by the age of just 26. He controlled the police force with bribes, and was responsible for many shootings, for which he always had an alibi. The most famous was the St Valentine's Day Massacre on 14 February 1929, when Al Capone organised the gunning down and killing of seven men, all but one of them from a rival gang. Capone was never put on trial for the crime because, as usual, he had an alibi.

Capone was finally jailed for tax evasion because the police couldn't prove that he was guilty of the murders, and he served eight years in prison from 1931.

Inez de Castro

Nationality:	**Spanish**
Born:	**About 1323**
Died:	**1355**

Horrible Deed: Inez was crowned Queen of Portugal after her death.

Horrible End: Inez de Castro was the girlfriend of the future King Pedro I of Portugal. Before he became king, he and Inez had children together and they married in secret in 1354. The following year Inez was murdered. When Pedro became king in 1357, he is supposed to have had Inez dug up and crowned Queen of Portugal. A procession of Portuguese nobles kissed the hand of the corpse. She had been dead for two years.

Quiz

Which Roman emperor was given the head of Pompey in a basket?

a) Julius Caesar
b) Tiberius
c) Claudius

Catherine II

Aka:	**Catherine The Great**
Nationality:	**German**
Born:	**1729**
Died:	**1796**
Occupation:	**Empress of Russia (1762-96)**

Horrible Deed: Cruelly torturing a rebel before his execution.

In 1773 Yemelyan Pugachov, an ex-army officer, began a rebellion against Catherine's rule. He gathered a large following and his troops were soon ready to march on Moscow. Catherine sent her own troops to put a stop to the rebellion. Pugachov was brought to Moscow in a cage, and had his arms and legs cut off before being beheaded.

Horrible End: Catherine died of a stroke whilst on the toilet.

King Charles VI

Aka:	**Charles the Mad, Charles the Well-beloved**
Nationality:	**French**
Born:	**1368**
Died:	**1422**
Occupation:	**King of France (1380-1422)**

Horrible Deeds: Killing four of his own men in a fit of madness, attacking doctors and servants, and having his wife's boyfriend tortured and killed.

Charles suffered from periods of madness throughout his life, despite (or perhaps because of) having holes drilled into his skull to relieve the condition. He believed that he was made of glass and might break at any moment, and refused to change his clothes or bathe. He would often attack doctors and servants who came near him when he was having an insane episode. Out riding with a group of knights one day he suddenly charged at his companions and killed four of them with his sword. Queen Isabeau, Charles's wife, was living separately from him, and had a boyfriend called Louis de Boisbourdon. During one of his sane periods, Charles had Louis tortured, strangled and thrown into the River Seine in a sack, while Queen Isabeau was banished.

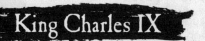

King Charles IX

Nationality: French

Born: 1550

Died: 1574

Occupation: King of France (1560-1574)

Horrible Deeds: Ordering the murder of his sister and brother-in-law and starting a massacre of thousands.

Persuaded by his mother, Catherine de Medici, Charles ordered the killing of his sister, *Marguerite de Valois* and her new husband on their wedding night. They escaped, but this marked the beginning of the Saint Bartholemew's Day Massacre of 1572, in which around 3,000 people were killed in Paris.

Claudius

Aka: Tiberius Claudius Augustus Germanicus

Nationality: Ancient Roman

Born: 10 BC

Died: AD 54

Occupation: Emperor of Rome (ruled AD 41-54)

Horrible Deeds: Killing thousands of prisoners, hundreds of citizens and one wife.

At the beginning of his reign, Claudius staged a mock naval battle in which 19,000 condemned prisoners took part on 100 ships. At the end of the entertainment only 100

C

prisoners had survived. Claudius had at least 35 politicians executed and more than 300 other wealthy citizens. His own wife, Messalina, was probably plotting against him and definitely had a boyfriend, so Claudius had her and her boyfriend put to death.

Horrible End: Claudius died in AD 54, believed to have been poisoned by his second wife, *Agrippina*.

Charlemagne

Aka:	**Charles I, Charles the Great**
Nationality:	**Frankish**
Born:	**About AD 742**
Died:	**AD 814**
Occupation:	**King of the Franks (768-814) King of the Lombards (774-814) and Emperor (800-814)**
Specialist Skills:	**Conquering.**

Horrible Deeds: Beheading thousands of Saxons and imposing harsh penalties.

After he became King of the Franks when he was 29, Charlemagne led a series of military campaigns to convert people to Christianity and extend his empire. He offered the conquered Saxons a choice: baptism as a Christian or death – and as a result he had 4,500 Saxons beheaded in one day. He also introduced the death penalty for eating meat during Lent.

Quiz

Which gangster was responsible for the Saint Valentine's Day Massacre?

a) Jesse James
b) Lucky Luciano
c) Al Capone

Shridhar Chillal

Nationality: Indian
Born: 1938
Occupation: Fingernail-grower and retired photographer

Horrible Deed: Growing incredibly long fingernails.

In 1998 the fingernails on Mr Chillal's left hand were measured at a total length of 6.15 metres, earning him a world record. Chillal tried to sell his fingernails for $200,000.

C

Christopher Columbus

Aka:	**Cristóbal Colón**
Nationality:	**Italian**
Born:	**1451**
Died:	**1506**
Occupation:	**Explorer**
Specialist Skills:	**Getting rich; being ruthless**

Horrible Deed: Enslaving and killing the Arawak people.

Christopher Columbus first visited the island of Haiti in 1492. He took about twenty of the Arawak people who lived there back to Spain with him. Only seven survived the voyage because they were treated so badly and because of the unhealthy conditions on board ship. In 1495 Columbus went back to Haiti and sent another 500 Arawaks to Spain as slaves. About 250 of them survived the journey.

Columbus continued to send many more slaves to Spain, but the Arawak people who remained on Haiti also had a horrible fate in store: they were forced to work hard to mine gold and provide food for Columbus and his troops, and were hardly able to feed themselves. Anyone who disobeyed suffered the punishment of having their ears, nose or hands cut off. Many of them decided to kill themselves rather than accept Columbus's rule. After two years, half the population of Arawak people on Haiti had died. Eventually, there were no Arawak people left on Haiti at all.

Captain James Cook

Nationality:	**English**
Born:	**1728**
Died:	**1779**
Occupation:	**Sea captain and explorer**

Horrible Deed: See Horrible End.

Horrible End: Cook had outstayed his welcome in Hawaii and a group of Hawaiians attacked him and some of his officers, hacking them to death with daggers and spears. After Cook was dead, his body was carried off by the Hawaiians. Cook's crew asked for their captain's body so that they could bury it at sea. Eventually two Hawaiians rowed out to Cook's ship with a package containing Captain Cook's thigh. The thigh received a decent burial, and a few days later more bits of Captain Cook were returned to the ship. The crew received a gruesome parcel containing: burnt bones, with a little flesh left on them; a pair of legs (but no feet); two arms; two hands (separate from the arms); the skull and the scalp (which had been separated from the skull and given a haircut). Cook's remains were finally buried at sea.

Mary Ann Cotton

Aka:	**Lady Rotten**
Nationality:	**English**
Born:	**1833**
Died:	**1873**
Occupation:	**District nurse and poisoner.**

Horrible Deeds: Murdering (probably) 36 people.

By the time she was suspected of poisoning her stepson, 21 people close to Mary Ann Cotton had died over the previous twenty years. It's thought that she was responsible for all of these plus another fifteen deaths. Among her victims were several boyfriends, a husband and two stepsons. She poisoned most of her victims with arsenic, which police discovered in the bodies they dug up as evidence for her trial. She was convicted of killing six people although she was suspected of many more murders

Horrible End: Mary Ann was hanged in Durham prison in 1873.

Crassus

Aka:	**Marcus Licinius Crassus**
Nationality:	**Ancient Roman**
Born:	**About 115 BC**
Died:	**53 BC**
Occupation:	**Politician and general.**
Specialist Skills:	**Getting rich.**

Horrible Deeds: Making money from unfortunate victims and crucifying rebel slaves.

Crassus became hugely wealthy. He made his money from property confiscated from wealthy people who'd been executed in *Sulla's* proscriptions. He also set up his own fire brigade – he'd buy a burning building from its owner at a cheap price, then get his firemen to put it out.

Crassus was in charge of the Roman troops who ended the slave rebellion led by *Spartacus*. He was responsible for crucifying 6,000 captured slaves alongside the the Appian Way, the road between Cappua and Rome.

Horrible End: Crassus wanted power as well as money and led an army against the Parthians, who defeated him and chopped off his head. The Parthian king, Orodes, is supposed to have poured molten gold into the dead Crassus's mouth, because he'd been thirsty for gold all his life.

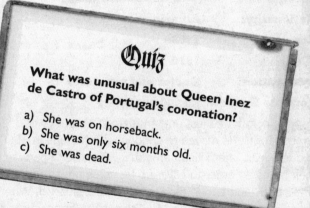

Quiz

What was unusual about Queen Inez de Castro of Portugal's coronation?

a) She was on horseback.
b) She was only six months old.
c) She was dead.

Dr Thomas Neill Cream

Aka:	**The Cross-eyed Lambeth Poisoner**
Nationality:	**Scottish**
Born:	**1850**
Died:	**1892**
Occupation:	**Doctor and poisoner.**

Horrible Deeds: Murdering at least five people.

C

While Cream was living in Chicago in 1881, he poisoned his girlfriend's husband with strychnine and was imprisoned for the crime. He was released ten years later and moved to Lambeth in London, where he poisoned at least four women, also with strychnine.

Horrible End: Cream was caught and hanged in 1892.

Dr Hawley Harvey Crippen

Nationality:	**American**
Born:	**1862**
Died:	**1910**
Occupation:	**Doctor and murderer**

Horrible Deed: Murdering his wife.

Crippen committed just one murder yet became world famous for it. He moved to London with his wife in 1900 and ten years later killed her with poison after a party at their home. In order to cover up his crime he cut up his wife's body and buried the pieces in the coal cellar. When police began investigating Mrs Crippen's disappearance, Dr Crippen and his girlfriend disguised themselves as father and son and boarded a ship to Canada. After they'd fled, Mrs Crippen's remains were discovered. The murderer was caught when the ship's captain became suspicious, and Crippen and his girlfriend were arrested and sent back to London.

Horrible End: Dr Crippen was hanged in 1910.

Oliver Cromwell

Nationality:	**English**
Born:	**1599**
Died:	**1658**
Occupation:	**Politician and army general**

Horrible Deeds: Killing thousands of people.

Cromwell led the Roundhead forces in the English Civil War against Charles I, who had his head chopped off. In 1649 Cromwell was sent to Ireland and began the conquest of the country by massacring 3,500 people in Drogheda, among them all the Catholic priests and friars in the town as well as other civilians.

Horrible End: When Cromwell died in 1658 he was leader of the English parliament, so he was given a grand funeral and his body was embalmed and buried in Westminster Abbey. Two years later the monarchy was restored and Cromwell was out of favour, so his corpse was dug up, taken to Tyburn gallows and hanged. Then the head was cut off and stuck on the end of an eight-metre pole on the roof of Westminster Hall. Twenty-four years later, in 1685, Cromwell's head was blown off in a gale and discovered by a soldier, who hid it in a chimney. Over the years the head was passed on from person to person, and appeared in a freak show in 1710 labelled "The Monster's Head". Cromwell had studied at Sydney Sussex College, Cambridge, and eventually, in 1960, the head was given to the college. It was finally buried somewhere in the college grounds (exactly where remains a secret).

C

George Armstrong Custer

Nationality:	**American**
Born:	**1839**
Died:	**1876**
Occupation:	**US cavalry officer**

Horrible Deed: Killing Cheyenne Indians.

Custer and his men attacked Cheyenne Chief Black Kettle's village on the Washita River, taking the village by surprise. All the men, women and children of the village were killed.

Horrible End: Instead of waiting for reinforcements, Custer attacked Chief Sitting Bull's encampment on the Little Big Horn River. Custer was killed and so were every one of the 264 men under his command. All of the dead US soldiers were scalped and mutilated by the Indians, except for Custer – no one knows why.

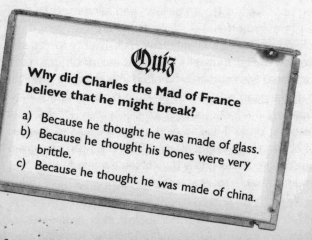

Quiz

Why did Charles the Mad of France believe that he might break?

a) Because he thought he was made of glass.

b) Because he thought his bones were very brittle.

c) Because he thought he was made of china.

Robert Damiens

Nationality:	French
Born:	1715
Died:	1757
Occupation:	Servant.

Horrible Deed: Damiens tried to stab Louis XV of France with a penknife but barely injured him.

Horrible End: Damiens' punishment was to be exectued by the gruesome method reserved for killers of kings (or attempted killers in his case): to have his limbs tied to horses which were then driven apart, tearing his body into pieces. First Damiens' legs were battered with sledgehammers, then his chest was torn open with red hot pincers and lead poured into the wounds. Next his hands and feet were tied to four horses, which were driven off in

D

different directions. Finally the different bits of Damiens' body were burnt at the stake. After his death, his house was burned to the ground, his brothers and sisters were ordered to change their names, and his father, wife, and daughter were banished from France.

Elaine Davidson

Nationality: **Scottish**

Horrible Deed: Elaine claims to have nearly 2,000 piercings on her body and holds the world record for the most piercings. She has nearly 200 piercings on her head and face alone.

Domitian

Aka:	**Caesar Domitianus Augustus**
Nationality:	**Ancient Roman**
Born:	**AD 51**
Died:	**AD 96**
Occupation:	**Emperor of Rome (AD 81-96)**

Horrible Deeds: Killing priestesses and politicians.

Domitian insisted on being addressed as "master and god". He had three priestesses (called Vestal Virgins) killed because they were accused of having boyfriends. In AD 90, the head of the Vestal Virgins, Cornelia, was buried alive on the orders of Domitian, and her alleged boyfriends were beaten to death. After a rebellion against him was discovered in AD 93, Domitian began a reign of terror, executing politicians he suspected of plotting against him.

Horrible End: After three years of terror, Domitian's opponents stabbed him to death. His wife, Domitia, was among the conspirators.

Alexander Douglas

Nationality:	Scottish
Born:	1767
Died:	1862
Occupation:	Tenth Duke of Hamilton

Horrible Deed: See Horrible End.

Horrible End: Douglas became obsessed with finding a suitably grand tomb for himself after his death. He paid a vast sum of money in 1852 for an Egyptian sarcophagus but found that he was too tall to fit inside it. When Douglas died he was embalmed and buried inside the tomb, but his feet had to be cut off and put into the sarcophagus separately so that he'd fit.

William Douglas

Nationality:	Scottish
Born:	About 1423
Died:	1440
Occupation:	Sixth Earl of Douglas

Horrible Deed: See Horrible End.

Horrible End: William Douglas and his younger brother

D

David were invited to the royal castle at Edinburgh by the ten-year-old King James II. The boys were served a black bull's head, which was the signal for them to be brutally murdered by the king's supporters. The incident became known as "The Black Dinner".

Quiz

Which Roman emperor made a rule allowing citizens to fart whenever they felt like it, even at the dinner table?

a) Caligula
b) Nero
c) Claudius

Draco

Nationality: Ancient Greek
Born: ? 7th century BC
Died: ? 7th century BC
Occupation: Athenian lawgiver

Horrible Deeds: Imposing harsh laws.

Draco's laws permitted enslavement for debt, and death seems to have been the penalty for almost all criminal offences, even minor ones. The historian Plutarch said that "Draco's laws were not written in ink but in blood."

Vlad Dracula

Aka:	**Vlad the Impaler**
Nationality:	**Wallachian**
Born:	**1431**
Died:	**1476**
Occupation:	**Prince of Wallachia (1456-1476)**
Specialist Skills:	**Being an evil tyrant**

Horrible Deeds: Impaling, disemboweling and boiling people.

When Vlad Dracula became the ruler of Wallachia (now in Romania) in 1456, he imposed horrible punishments. For a wide range of crimes (which included stealing, lying, or just being someone Vlad didn't like), the punishment was impalement. This meant that victims were speared with a stake then hoisted upright – an extremely painful and slow way to die.

Vlad once invited all the sick, old and poor people of the land to a great feast. After they'd eaten, Vlad asked them whether they would like to be free from care and hunger for ever. When they replied that they would, Vlad boarded up the windows and doors to the feasting hall and set fire to it. No one survived.

While Vlad was in charge, many thousands of people were impaled, burned alive, boiled, disemboweled, tortured and kept in slavery. It's said that he liked to set up a banquet table and eat dinner while he watched his victims die. There were also rumours that Vlad drank the blood of some of his victims. Impaling remained Vlad's favourite punishment and, after his death in battle in 1476, he became known as Vlad the Impaler.

Answer: c. Claudius thought it was bad for people to hold in their farts and passed the law out of concern for their health.

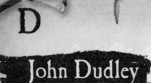

D

John Dudley

Nationality:	**English**
Born:	**1502**
Died:	**1553**
Occupation:	**Duke of Northumberland**

Horrible Deeds: Dudley tried to put the young Lady Jane Grey on the throne instead of Queen Mary I, and met with a horrible end.

Horrible End: Mary had Dudley hanged, drawn and quartered. This meant that he was dragged to the place of execution, hanged until almost dead, then disembowelled and his insides burned in front of his eyes, then beheaded and the body cut into four pieces. Mary added an extra bonus in Dudley's case by having his heart cut out and flung in his face as part of the execution. Lady Jane Grey was executed too: she was beheaded.

HELP ME

Edward I

Aka:	**The Hammer of the Scots; Edward Longshanks**
Nationality:	**English**
Born:	**1239**
Died:	**1307**
Occupation:	**King of England (1272-1307)**

Horrible Deed: Massacring an entire town.

Edward was determined to conquer the Scottish people and take the crown of Scotland for himself. He decided to set an example with the town of Berwick: he destroyed much of the town, had everybody killed and gave orders for the bodies to be left in the streets to rot, to remind everyone of his power.

Edward defeated the Scottish rebel *William Wallace* and

E

had him hanged, drawn and quartered. As was the usual practice, Edward sent the various pieces of Wallace's body to be displayed at different castles in England and Scotland, and he had Wallace's head stuck on a pole on London Bridge.

Horrible End: After Edward's death his body was boiled to extract the bones, so that they could be carried into battle.

Quiz

1. Which famous leader's head ended up in a freak show labelled "The Monster's Head"?
   a) Alexander the Great's.
   b) Atilla the Hun's.
   c) Oliver Cromwell's.

2. Whom did Dr Crippen murder?
   a) His patients.
   b) His wife.
   c) His receptionist.

Edward V

Nationality:	**English**
Born:	1470
Died:	? 1483
Occupation:	King of England (April - June 1483)

Horrible End: Edward came to the throne when he was

twelve but in June 1483 his uncle, the future Richard III, got a bishop to declare that Edward's mother and father had never been married, which meant that Edward couldn't be king. Richard then had Edward imprisoned in the Tower of London with his younger brother. It's thought Richard had the two princes murdered there, probably in 1483.

Ken Edwards

Nationality: English
Born: ?
Occupation: Entertainer

Horrible Deeds: Eating cockroaches and sharing his tights with rats.

Ken Edwards ate 36 cockroaches in one minute in 2001, earning him a world record. His stage act involves wearing a pair of tights and stuffing them with 47 live rats.

Elagabalus

Aka: Caesar Marcus Aurelius Antoninus Augustus
Born: 204
Died: 222
Occupation: Roman Emperor (218-222)

Horrible Deeds: Elagabalus was an unpopular emperor due to his extravagance and the fact that he executed anyone who criticised his strange ways. He met a horrible end at the hands of his enemies.

Answer: 1.c 2.b

E

Horrible End: Elagabalus was killed in a toilet, beheaded along with his mother, dragged through the streets of Rome and dumped in the River Tiber.

Elizabeth I

Aka:	**Good Queen Bess**
Nationality:	**English**
Born:	**1533**
Died:	**1603**
Occupation:	**Queen of England (1558-1603)**

Horrible Deeds: Executing hundreds of people.

Elizabeth executed 200 people just for being Catholic (although only four of them were burned - her sister *Mary I* had burned nearly 300 in only five years). Other executions included her cousin, Mary Queen of Scots and her favourite courtier, the Earl of Essex. She imprisoned Walter Raleigh and his wife just for getting married to one another.

Quiz

Which famous explorer was chopped to bits in Hawaii?

a) Christopher Columbus
b) Marco Polo
c) Captain Cook

Eric XIV

Nationality:	Swedish
Born:	1533
Died:	1577
Occupation:	King of Sweden (1560-1569)

Horrible Deeds: Executing people.

Like his father *Gustav I*, Eric had a violent temper. He would condemn servants to be executed for no reason at all – sometimes simply because they annoyed him. Anyone whispering or coughing in his presence might be accused of plotting and put to death.

Eric was worried that someone might try to take his throne so he executed and imprisoned several nobles. One of them, Nils Sture, was imprisoned with the rest of his family at Uppsala Castle when Eric arrived and stabbed him to death himself, leaving orders for the rest of the Stures to be executed immediately. Eric's old tutor was concerned for Eric and went after him – Eric killed him too.

In 1569 Eric was kicked off the throne and imprisoned by his younger brother John.

Horrible End: Eric was poisoned with arsenic in 1577 on the orders of his brother.

Answer: c

Guy Fawkes

Aka:	**Guido Fawkes, John Johnson**
Nationality:	**English**
Born:	**1570**
Died:	**1606**
Occupation:	**Soldier, explosives expert and gunpowder plotter.**

Horrible Deed: Caught red-handed about to blow up the Houses of Parliament.

Guy Fawkes was the explosives expert in the Gunpowder Plot. He was caught with 36 barrels of gunpowder in the cellar of the Houses of Parliament, with which he intended to blow up King James I and the rest of the government.

Horrible End: Fawkes was horribly tortured until he confessed (he could barely sign his name on the confession). A committee was set up to try and think of a really horrible punishment for him, but they couldn't think of a worse one than the traditional hanging, drawing and quartering, so that's what Fawkes got.

King Ferdinand and Queen Isabella

Nationality: Spanish
Born: Ferdinand 1452, Isabella 1451
Died: Ferdinand 1516, Isabella 1504
Occupation: King and Queen of Spain

Horrible Deed: Responsible for the Spanish Inquisition.

Ferdinand and Isabella were so keen on being Catholic that they were known as the Catholic Monarchs. They wanted everyone else to be just as Catholic as they were, so they offered all non-Catholics a choice between converting to their religion or being kicked out of the country. They started the Spanish Inquisition in 1478 to make sure people were Catholic enough (but really they just used it to punish people horribly – see *Tomas Torquemada*). Isabella is supposed to have vowed to wear the same clothes until the Moors were conquered – the Moors were driven out in 1492, four years after she made the vow.

Oliverotti da Fermo

Nationality: Italian
Born: About 1475
Died: 1502
Occupation: Soldier, aristocrat and murderer.

F

Horrible Deed: Murdering his dinner party guests, including his own uncle.

Oliverotti returned to his home town, Fermo, after 15 years away working as a soldier. He invited his Uncle Giovanni, Prince of Fermo, to a banquet with other important people of the town. Oliverotti wanted to run Fermo himself. So, during the banquet he called his guests to a more private room, then he and his "guard of honour" – 100 trained killers – murdered the lot of them.

Horrible End: Oliverotti ended up being killed himself, strangled by *Cesare Borgia*.

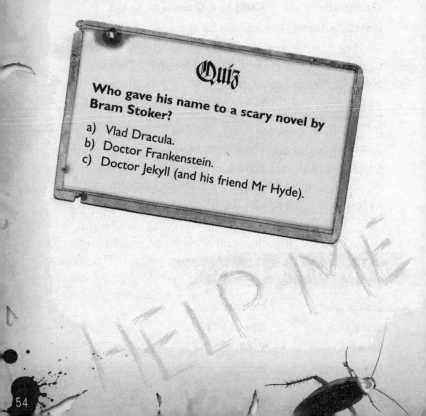

Quiz

Who gave his name to a scary novel by Bram Stoker?

a) Vlad Dracula.
b) Doctor Frankenstein.
c) Doctor Jekyll (and his friend Mr Hyde).

G

Gelon

Aka:	**The Tyrant of Syracuse**
Nationality:	**Ancient Greek**
Born:	**540 BC**
Died:	**478 BC**
Occupation:	**Ruler of Gela and Syracuse.**

Horrible Deed: As well as the usual tyrannical activities of conquering and enslaving people, Gelon suffered from terrible bad breath. When one of his girlfriends told him about it, he shouted at his wife for not telling him before. His wife defended herself by saying that she didn't know any other men and had assumed they must all smell as bad as Gelon.

Answer: a

G

Robert of Geneva

Aka:	**Pope Clement VII, The Butcher of Cesena**
Nationality:	**Swiss**
Born:	**1342**
Died:	**1394**
Occupation:	**Pope**

Horrible Deeds: Ordering the massacre of thousands of people.

Robert became Pope in 1378, elected by a group who opposed *Urban VI*, the Mad Pope. The year before, Robert had given the order to execute 4,000 people in the town of Cesena in northern Italy, in order to stop a rebellion. He was nicknamed 'The Butcher of Cesena' because of this, but it didn't stop him becoming Pope.

George II

Nationality:	**German**
Born:	**1683**
Died:	**1760**
Occupation:	**King of Great Britain (1727-1760)**

Horrible End: George died after having a fit and falling off the toilet. (See also *Catherine the Great*.)

George IV

Nationality:	**English**
Born:	**1762**
Died:	**1830**
Occupation:	**King of United Kingdom of Great Britain and Ireland (ruled 1820 to 1830)**

Horrible End: When George died, he was so fat that his body only just fitted inside its coffin. The coffin began to expand and threatened to explode, so holes had to be drilled into it to allow the gases trapped inside to escape.

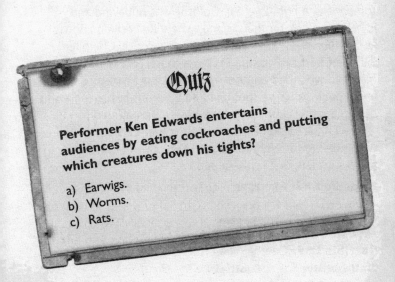

Quiz

Performer Ken Edwards entertains audiences by eating cockroaches and putting which creatures down his tights?

a) Earwigs.
b) Worms.
c) Rats.

G

Crawford Goldsby

Aka:	**Cherokee Bill**
Nationality:	**American**
Born:	**1876**
Died:	**1896**
Occupation:	**Outlaw**

Horrible Deeds: Shooting and killing at least seven people.

Crawford Goldsby's first victim was his brother-in-law, whom he shot dead when he was just twelve years old (later he killed a different brother-in-law). After shooting someone in a fight in a bar, Goldsby was outlawed and joined the Cook brothers' gang, where he became known as Cherokee Bill. Soon after joining the Cooks, Cherokee Bill killed Deputy Houston during a chase, and killed two men and wounded another when robbing a railway depot and a bank. After he shot dead an innocent bystander during another robbery, a large reward was offered for Cherokee Bill, dead or alive. He was caught and convicted of murder. An attempted escape from prison resulted in another victim, one of the guards.

Horrible End: Cherokee Bill was executed in 1896.

George Gordon

Nationality:	**Scottish**
Born:	**1514**
Died:	**1562**
Occupation:	**Earl of Huntly**

Horrible Deed: Leading a rebellion against Mary Queen of Scots, which was defeated at the Battle of Corrichie, and meeting a horrible end.

Horrible End: George Gordon died on the battlefield, but in order for his lands to be confiscated he had to be convicted of treason. So his body was preserved with spices to stop it from putrefying and was then taken to Edinburgh. There, Gordon's corpse was put on trial. Not surprisingly, he was found guilty of treason. The body was then taken away and beheaded.

Sir Robert Graham

Nationality:	**Scottish**
Born:	**?**
Died:	**1437**
Occupation:	**Noble**

Horrible Deed: Assassinated King James I of Scotland.

Sir Robert Graham was among the many Scots who opposed the king because he'd executed some nobles. While King James was giving a party at his castle in Perth, Graham arrived, leading a group of conspirators including *Walter, Earl of Atholl*, and murdered the king, who was hiding in a sewer. Graham was tracked down by the queen soon after the murder.

Horrible End: Graham was carried naked in a cart through the streets of Edinburgh, with his right hand nailed to a post, while torturers prodded and stabbed him with red-hot irons and knives. The next day he was executed, though first the blanket he'd wrapped around himself was ripped from him, opening the wounds he'd received the day before. Before he died, Graham's son was executed in front of him.

Gustav I

Nationality: Swedish
Born: 1496
Died: 1560
Occupation: King of Sweden (1523-1560)
Horrible Deeds: Attacking and (in one case) killing people.

Gustav was prone to violent rages. He once chased one of his secretaries wielding a dagger, pulled his daughter's hair out by the roots, and beat his goldsmith to death for taking the day off without permission.

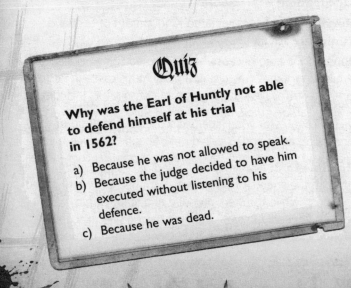

Quiz

Why was the Earl of Huntly not able to defend himself at his trial in 1562?

a) Because he was not allowed to speak.
b) Because the judge decided to have him executed without listening to his defence.
c) Because he was dead.

Professor Gunther von Hagens

Nationality: German

Born: 1945

Occupation: Doctor

Horrible Deed: Exhibiting preserved human corpses.

In 1977 Professor von Hagens discovered a method of preserving dead bodies called "plastination", which meant that dead bodies could be displayed at medical conferences. Later he realised that the general public might also be interested, and Bodyworlds, his exhibition of preserved human bodies, first opened to the public in 1995. Von Hagens has made plans to be plastinated himself when he dies.

Answer: c

H

John George Haigh

Aka:	**The Acid Bath Murderer**
Nationality:	**English**
Born:	**1910**
Died:	**1949**
Occupation:	**Engineer and murderer**

Horrible Deeds: Killed nine people and got rid of their bodies in a vat of acid.

Haigh invited a woman he knew to his factory, where he shot her dead and dissolved her body in a drum of sulphuric acid. He reported her disappearance to the police, who became suspicious and found evidence of the killing at Haigh's factory. Haigh then admitted to having killed eight other people in the same way, three of them members of the same family.

Horrible End: Haigh was executed in 1949.

Sir Henry Halford

Nationality:	**English**
Born:	**1766**
Died:	**1844**
Occupation:	**Royal Surgeon**

Horrible Deeds: Used the bone of a dead king as a salt cellar.

In 1649, Charles I of England was beheaded and buried at Windsor Castle. In 1813 Sir Henry Halford was asked to

perform an autopsy on Charles I's body, during which he secretly stole one of the dead king's vertebrae. Sir Henry liked to shock people at his dinner parties by using the bone as a gruesome salt cellar. He kept the vertebra for 30 years, until Queen Victoria found out about it and demanded its immediate return to Charles I's skeleton.

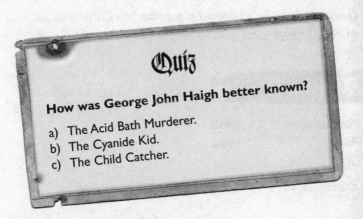

Quiz

How was George John Haigh better known?

a) The Acid Bath Murderer.
b) The Cyanide Kid.
c) The Child Catcher.

John Wesley Hardin

Nationality:	**American**
Born:	**1853**
Died:	**1895**
Occupation:	**Outlaw**

Horrible Deeds: Shooting and killing at least thirteen people.

At the age of fourteen John Hardin stabbed a school mate and at fifteen he shot a man dead. On the run after the

H

murder, he killed one (and maybe more) of the soldiers who were chasing him. Hardin went on to kill at least another ten people, including a deputy sheriff, a police captain and a Texas ranger.

Hardin was sent to prison for 25 years for murdering the deputy sheriff and was released in 1894. He became a lawyer, having studied the law in prison.

Horrible End: Hardin hired a gunman to kill the husband of his girlfriend – the gunman shot Hardin instead.

William Hare

Nationality:	**Irish**
Born:	**1790**
Died:	**1860**
Occupation:	**Lodging-house owner and murderer**

Horrible Deeds: Body-snatching and murdering at least fifteen people.

William Hare began body-snatching with his partner *William Burke* and selling the corpses to surgeons for medical experiments. Not finding a good enough supply of bodies from graveyards, the pair began murdering people to keep up with the surgeons' demand. They were caught, but Hare and his girlfriend Maggie Laird gave evidence against Burke and his girlfriend in order to escape the death penalty.

Horrible End: Hare ended up begging in the streets of London, where he died in poverty.

Henry V

Nationality:	**English**
Born:	**1387**
Died:	**1422**
Occupation:	**King of England (1413-1422)**

Horrible Deeds: Killing hundreds of prisoners of war.

Henry V fought in the Hundred Years War between England and France. After a great English victory at Agincourt, Henry had all of the French prisoners – about 1,800 of them – ruthlessly killed.

Horrible End: Henry died of a fever while he was in France. His body was boiled up until the flesh fell off the bones, then his skeleton was sent back to England for burial.

Henry IV

Nationality:	**English**
Born:	**1366**
Died:	**1413**
Occupation:	**King of England (1399-1413)**

Horrible Deed: Henry IV was horribly afflicted by a huge growth underneath his nose, seeping sores all over his body, and headlice, which were hopping and wriggling through his hair as the crown was put on his head at his coronation.

H

Henry VIII

Nationality:	**English**
Born:	**1491**
Died:	**1547**
Occupation:	**King of England (1509-1547)**

Horrible Deeds: Having thousands of people executed.

Henry VIII had tens of thousands of people executed during the 38 years of his reign, and probably had more people executed for their beliefs than any other monarch. Hundreds of people died because they wouldn't acknowledge Henry as Head of the Church instead of the Pope.

Henry took a personal interest in some cases: he made an example of ten Carthusian monks, who were chained up to pillars in filthy conditions in Newgate prison and left to die slowly of starvation. He wanted to execute Cardinal Reginald Pole but he'd left the country, so Henry had seven people executed just for being connected to Pole, including his brother and his elderly mother.

Henry decided that he'd get rid of the monasteries in England and confiscate their wealth and land. There was a peaceful protest about this in the north of England called the Pilgrimage of Grace. Henry said he'd listen to the protestors' complaints but instead he had hundreds of them executed – he hanged the monks at one monastery from the steeple of their church.

Henry is probably most famous for marrying six wives and having two of them beheaded, Anne Boleyn and Catherine Howard (who was just seventeen when she was executed).

He divorced his first wife, Catherine of Aragon, and when she died he held a big party.

Horrible End: In the last months of his life, Henry had to be carried everywhere in a chair because of the smelly, seeping ulcers on his legs. He died a slow and painful death.

Quiz

Sir Henry Halford secretly stole a bone from Charles I's skeleton. How did he make use of it?

a) As a salt cellar.
b) As a walking stick.
c) He gave it to his dog.

Herod

Aka:	**Herod the Great**
Nationality:	**Judaean**
Born:	**73 BC**
Died:	**4 BC**
Occupation:	**King of Judaea (37-4 BC)**

Horrible Deeds: Slaughtering the children of Bethlehem, as well as various members of his own family.

The first member of the family to be killed by Herod was his brother-in-law, Aristobulus – he was too popular for Herod's liking. Then he became jealous of his wife, Miriam, and suspected that she was having an affair with his uncle, Joseph. He had both Miriam and Joseph killed and later he murdered Miriam's mother and grandfather. Later, Herod also killed the two sons he had with Miriam, because Antipater, Herod's eldest son, accused them of plotting against Herod. It wasn't long before Herod found Antipater guilty of plotting to poison him, and he was executed too.

Herod is most famous for ordering the death of all the male infants in Bethlehem under two years old, because it had been prophesied that one of them would become king of the Jews.

On his deathbed, Herod heard that a group of students had torn down a Roman symbol: he had them and their teacher burned alive. Then he ordered that all the men of the most important families in the country should be imprisoned in Jericho – when he died, he wanted them all to be executed so that the whole country would be in deep mourning. Thankfully, his orders weren't followed.

James Butler Hickok

Aka:	**Wild Bill Hickok**
Nationality:	**American**
Born:	**1837**
Died:	**1876**
Occupation:	**US Marshal, army scout and gunman**

Horrible Deeds: Shooting and killing at least eight men

(though not as many as he claimed).

Wild Bill Hickok earned his nickname when he shot dead three men while working as a wagon master in Montana. In 1865, after an argument over a card game, Hickok won a quick-draw duel when he shot and killed his opponent. He fuelled his reputation by claiming to have killed more than a hundred men, though this certainly wasn't true. He was made Sheriff of Hays City in Kansas in 1868, but after shooting two men dead within his first year in the job, people became alarmed and the town replaced him with his deputy. Two years later he lost his job as a marshal after he'd killed two more men.

Horrible End: Wild Bill Hickok was shot dead while playing poker. His murderer, James McCall, said he'd killed Hickok in revenge for killing his brother, and was hanged for the crime. The cards Hickok was holding when he died included two black aces and two black eights – this hand is still known as "dead man's hand".

Hippocrates

Nationality:	**Ancient Greek**
Born:	**About 460 BC**
Died:	**About 377 BC**
Occupation:	**Doctor**
Specialist Skills:	**Curing people (many of his practices were very effective).**

Horrible Deed: Hippocrates taught that the earwax, snot, urine and vomit of sick patients should be tasted by the doctor to discover what was wrong with them.

Louise Hollis

Nationality: American

Horrible Deed: Growing incredibly long toenails.

Californian grandmother Louise Hollis holds the record for the world's longest toenails. When they were officially measured in 1991 the combined length of her ten toenails was 2.21 metres. She spends two days a week caring for the nails. (See also *Shridhar Chillal*.)

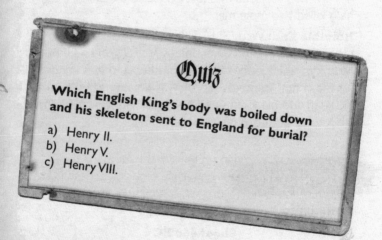

Quiz

Which English King's body was boiled down and his skeleton sent to England for burial?

a) Henry II.
b) Henry V.
c) Henry VIII.

Paul Hunn

Nationality: English

Born: 1969

Occupation: Solicitor's clerk and burper.

Horrible Deeds: Burping incredibly loudly.

H

Paul Hunn is officially the world's loudest burper. His record-breaking burp measured 118.1 decibels – as loud as a pneumatic drill.

Horror Rating: 2/10

Shihan Hussaini

Nationality: Indian

Born: 1965

Occupation: Artist

Horrible Deed: Painting portraits with his own blood.

Hussaini used his own blood to paint 56 portraits of Indian politician Jayaram Jayalalitha. He drew up to 80 millilitres of his blood every day for twenty days, then added chemicals to stop it from clotting and exposed it to sunlight to create different shades.

Matthew Hopkins

Nationality: English

Born: ?

Died: 1647

Occupation: Witchfinder General

Horrible Deeds: Forced hundreds of people to confess to being witches, then had them burned alive.

Matthew Hopkins had such a good track record at finding "witches" (mostly poor old ladies) that he was made Witchfinder General. He travelled around England finding

Answer: b

H

his victims and was highly paid for every witch he discovered. His main method of finding out whether or not someone was a witch was to put her in a pond – if she floated she was guilty and should be put to death; if she sank she was innocent (but drowned). Hopkins tried to make sure he arranged the accused person's clothing so that she floated. The punishment for being a witch was usually to be burned at the stake. It's thought Hopkins found and executed more than 200 "witches".

Horrible End: Matthew Hopkins was eventually accused of being a wizard himself. He was put in a pond and he floated – we don't know exactly what happened to him but he was probably hanged on the spot.

Quiz

What was the dying wish of Herod the Great?

a) For the men of the most important families in Judea to be executed.

b) For a month-long torture festival at his palace.

c) For his body to be embalmed and displayed on his throne for ever.

Qin Shi Huang

Aka:	**The First Emperor, The Tiger Emperor**
Nationality:	**Chinese**
Born:	**260 BC**
Died:	**210 BC**
Occupation:	**King of the State of Qin (247 BC - 221 BC), and first Emperor of a unified China (221 BC - 210 BC)**
Specialist Skills:	**Uniting China; building the Great Wall and the Terracotta Army (8,000 life-size terracotta warriors made for his tomb).**

Horrible Deeds: Killing scholars, burning books and working people to death.

Qin Shi Huang forced 500,000 labourers (mostly captured enemies) to work on the Great Wall of China. He stationed troops to oversee the workers, and imposed harsh conditions and punishments. Seven out of ten of them (350,000 people) died from hunger and overwork.

The First Emperor took a dislike to a group of scholars called Confucians and had 460 of them executed by burying them up to their necks and then chopping their heads off. Then he burned all books by the scholars as well as any others he didn't like. He also made a rule that anyone expressing a political opinion should be killed, along with their entire family.

Horrible End: Qin Shi Huang died on his way back from a tour of eastern China. The Prime Minister, Li Si, feared an uprising if his death became known before they arrived at

Answer: a. Herod's wish wasn't granted.

the capital, which wouldn't be for two months, so he kept the Emperor's death a secret. Li Si had "discussions" with the dead emperor in his carriage every day so that no one suspected. To hide the smell of his decomposing body, two carriages containing fish went before and after the emperor's carriage.

John Hunter

Nationality:	**English**
Born:	**1728**
Died:	**1793**
Occupation:	**Surgeon**

Horrible Deeds: Body-snatching.

John Hunter was interested in dissecting dead bodies but, since there weren't many people who were happy for their bodies to be used as medical experiments when they died, corpses were in short supply. Hunter robbed graves himself in his early days as a surgeon – either from fresh graves or from the gallows – and later he paid other body-snatchers to get bodies for him.

Hunter was especially keen to get his hands on the dead body of Charles Byrne, who was nearly two-and-a-half metres tall and known as "the Irish Giant". Hunter suggested to Byrne that he would pay him while he lived in return for his body after he died, but Byrne was horrified and did everything he could to avoid Hunter experimenting on his dead body. When Byrne died, Hunter sneakily arranged with the undertaker to swap Byrne's body with stones. Once he had the body, Hunter cut it up and boiled it to remove the flesh. Today, Charles Byrne's skeleton is on display at the Hunterian Museum at the Royal College of Surgeons in London. Also exhibited at the museum are the kidney of Hunter's father-in-law and the bladder of his local vicar.

Horrible End: Hunter insisted that his body be used for dissection by his students after his death, and he got his wish. He also asked for his heart to be removed and kept in his museum, but for some reason that never happened.

Quiz

What was unusual about the portraits by Shihan Hussaini of politician Jayaram Jayalalitha?

a) They included real hair from Jayaram Jayalalitha's head.

b) They were painted in the artist's blood.

c) They were painted on paper made from elephant dung.

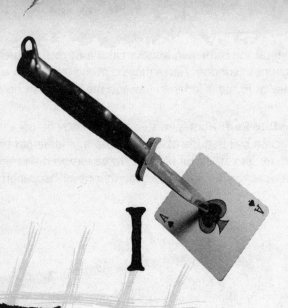

Ivan IV

Aka:	**Ivan the Terrible**
Nationality:	**Russian**
Born:	**1530**
Died:	**1584**
Occupation:	**Grand Prince of Moscow (1533-84) and Tsar of Russia (1547-84)**
Specialist Skills:	**Being an evil tyrant**

Horrible Deeds: Torturing and killing thousands.

Ivan showed his nasty side from a young age: he liked to drop dogs from the 60-metre-tall towers of the Kremlin palace in Moscow. After his wife died in 1560, Ivan became paranoid and began torturing and imprisoning anyone he found suspicious. Ivan liked to witness torture and would often go to the dungeons to watch. He would sometimes give detailed instructions about methods of torture, some of which were based on descriptions of Hell in the Bible. Ivan created a private army of the most brutal thugs he could find, the Oprichniks, to carry out the torture and executions for him. They soon terrorised the whole of Russia.

Ivan suspected that the people of Novgorod were plotting a rebellion, so in 1570 he had the Oprichniks barricade the town. Every day hundreds of townspeople were brought to Novgorod's Great Square and most of them were tortured and killed – some were impaled, burned or skinned alive, many were mutilated before being killed. Every day at least 600 people were murdered in the square, some days as many as 1500. The Volkhov river became so full of bodies that it flooded. It's thought that somewhere between 17,000 and 60,000 Novgorod townspeople were killed during the Oprichniks' reign of terror. In Moscow the same year Ivan held a public torture festival in which hundreds of prisoners were tortured and executed until the whole city stank because of the dead bodies.

There are many other examples of Ivan's cruelty: he killed two of his eight wives and at least one of his sons – he bashed his son Ivan's head in during an argument, and might have drowned another. He also nailed a foreign ambassador's hat to his head (because he wouldn't take it off), and set alight the hair and beards of two Russian nobles after dousing them in alcohol. He once invited some starving peasants to his house to be fed, then had them killed and thrown into the river as a joke.

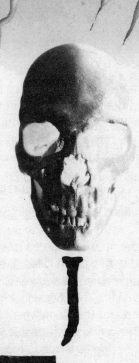

Jack the Ripper

Nationality: ?

Born: ?

Died: ?

Occupation: Murderer

Horrible Deeds: Between August and November 1888, five women were murdered in Whitechapel, East London. The murders were especially gruesome and police were convinced that they were the work of one person, to whom they gave the nickname Jack the Ripper. The murderer was never caught, and the murders stopped as suddenly as they had started. Suspects for the murders included Queen Victoria's grandson.

James II

Nationality:	**Scottish**
Born:	**1430**
Died:	**1460**
Occupation:	**King of Scotland (1437-1460)**

Horrible Deeds: Killing various members of the Douglas familiy.

King James and his supporters thought that the Douglas family had too much power. The sixth Earl of Douglas and his brother were invited to dinner, but when the infamous Black Dinner was served it was as a signal for the two Douglas boys to be murdered.

Twelve years later, in 1452, James invited William, the eighth Earl of Douglas to dinner at Stirling Castle. During the meal, James leaned over and stabbed him half to death – his servants finished William off.

Horrible End: James defeated the English at Roxburgh Castle. After the victory a canon was fired in celebration but exploded and a piece of wood chopped James's leg off. He bled to death.

Frank and Jesse James

Nationality:	**American**
Born:	**1843 (Frank) and 1847 (Jesse)**
Died:	**1915 (Frank) and 1882 (Jesse)**
Occupation:	**Outlaws**

Horrible Deeds: Stealing and killing.

J

The James brothers led a gang that robbed banks and trains. They robbed their first bank in 1866, shooting and killing an unarmed student as they rode out of the town (they killed many people for no reason at all in the course of their crimes). The brothers were pursued by the Pinkerton Detective Agency. Jessie James hanged one of the Pinkerton agents from a tree when he caught him, with a sign round his neck reading "Compliments of the James boys". Most of the gang was killed when a bank robbery went wrong, but Jesse set up another one.

Horrible End: One of the new gang members, Bob Ford, shot Jesse James in the back in return for reward money. Frank James died of old age.

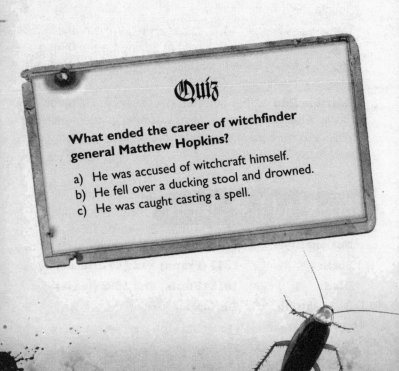

Quiz

What ended the career of witchfinder general Matthew Hopkins?

a) He was accused of witchcraft himself.
b) He fell over a ducking stool and drowned.
c) He was caught casting a spell.

Judge George Jeffreys

Aka:	**The Bloody Judge**
Nationality:	**Welsh**
Born:	**1648**
Died:	**1689**
Occupation:	**Judge**
Specialist Skills:	**Binge drinking; being completely unjust**

Horrible Deeds: Enthusiastically sentencing people to be hanged or transported, and accepting bribes.

Jeffreys drank excessively, often turning up in court either with a hangover or still drunk, routinely abused and ridiculed defendants, and dealt out the harshest punishments. He became most famous for his part in the Bloody Assizes – the trial of supposed followers of the Duke of Monmouth, who'd been trying to overthrow King James II. Jeffreys happily sentenced 74 people to be hanged in Dorset, and 253 people to be hanged, drawn and quartered in Somerset, leaving bits of bodies on display throughout the countryside. At the same time he earned money by accepting bribes from the victims.

Horrible End: When James II's government was overthrown in 1688, Jeffreys had no one to protect him and tried to leave the country disguised as a sailor. He was arrested, imprisoned in the Tower of London and died there a few months later.

Answer: a

J

Juana I

Aka: **Juana The Mad**

Nationality: **Spanish**

Born: **1479**

Died: **1555**

Occupation: **Queen of Castile (from 1504) and of Aragon (from 1516)**

Specialist Skills: **Concocting love potions (with limited success); being mad.**

Horrible Deed: Travelling about with a corpse in a coffin.

The daughter of *King Ferdinand* and *Queen Isabella*, Juana only went completely mad after she married Philip the Handsome, and particularly after his death - which may have been caused by drinking one of Juana the Mad's love potions. Instead of burying her husband, Juana kept Philip's dead body with her, travelling about Spain with it in a coffin so that she could keep an eye on the rotting remains.

Quiz

Which Russian ruler massacred the people of Novgorod?

a) Ivan the Terrible.

b) Peter the Great.

c) Catherine the Great.

Edward Kelly

Aka:	**Ned Kelly**
Nationality:	**Australian**
Born:	**1855**
Died:	**1880**
Occupation:	**Outlaw**

Horrible Deeds: Stealing horses and killing policemen.

In 1877 Ned Kelly shot a policeman who was arresting his brother for stealing horses. The policeman recovered, but the brothers were now wanted men and fled to the Australian bush where they were joined by two friends. The Kelly gang lived by stealing horses and property – their daring robberies made them heroes to some people. By 1878 they had shot and killed three policemen.

In 1880 the gang was surrounded by police. Ned Kelly wore

Answer: a

a home-made suit of armour to withstand the police bullets, but he was wounded and captured. The rest of the gang was killed.

Horrible End: Ned Kelly was hanged at Melbourne jail soon after his capture.

Susanna Kennedy

Nationality:	English
Born:	1696
Died:	1787
Occupation:	Countess of Eglintoune

Horrible Deed: Keeping hundreds of rats.

The Countess's pet rats had the free run of her home. She liked to eat dinner with them and would call them to the dining table by tapping on an oak panel. The rats would join her at the table then leave obediently at her command.

Quiz

Who was Juana the Mad's husband?

a) Philip the Sane.
b) Philip the Handsome.
c) Philip the Nervous.

R.I.P.

Genghis Khan

Aka:	**Temujin**
Nationality:	**Mongolian**
Born:	**1155, 1162 or 1167**
Died:	**1227**
Occupation:	**Warrior and ruler**
Specialist Skills:	**Plundering, pillaging and conquering.**

Horrible Deeds: Slaughtering millions.

Genghis Khan ruthlessly disposed of his enemies during his rise to power. Once he was in charge, he united the nomadic Mongolian tribes under his rule and began the first of many bloody invasions that led to his huge Mongol Empire. After defeating the Tatars in battle, he killed any of them who was taller than a cart axle - leaving only the younger children, who might grow up to be loyal to the Mongols.

Genghis Khan's army became famous for its ruthlessness and destruction. We don't know exactly how many people were slaughtered by Genghis's conquering hordes, but several million people died.

L

Michel Lotito

Aka: **Monsieur Mangetout**

Nationality: **French**

Born: **1950**

Occupation: **Entertainer**

Horrible Deeds: Eating metal and glass.

Monsieur Mangetout – "Mr Eat Everything" in English – has been eating metal and glass since 1959. He regularly eats 900 grammes of metal per day, and his diet has included cutlery, razors, bicycles, televisions, shopping trolleys and a Cessner light aircraft (which took him two years to eat).

L

Louis XIV

Aka:	**Louis the Great, The Sun King, Le Roi Soleil**
Nationality:	**French**
Born:	**1638**
Died:	**1715**
Occupation:	**King of France (1643-1715)**

Horrible Deed: Taking only three baths in his whole life.

The only times Louis had a bath were when he was baptized, when one of his girlfriends insisted (and who can blame her?), and when he was told by a doctor to soak a boil on his bottom that had just been lanced. Louis wasn't unusual: most Europeans at the time hardly ever had baths or washed.

James Lowther

Aka:	**The Bad Earl**
Nationality:	**English**
Born:	**1736**
Died:	**1802**
Occupation:	**First Earl of Lonsdale**

Horrible Deed: Keeping his dead wife in his dining room.

Lowther earned his nickname of The Bad Earl because of his fits of temper, miserliness and appalling treatment of his tenants. One of the only people he treated well was his wife, who died young. Lowther had her body embalmed and placed in a glass-topped coffin, which he used as a piece of furniture in his dining room.

Quiz

Piero Manzoni's artwork includes ninety cans of which substance?

a) Earwax.
b) Poo.
c) Baked beans.

Salvatore Lucania

Aka:	**Lucky Luciano**
Nationality:	**Italian-American**
Born:	**1896**
Died:	**1962**
Occupation:	**Gangster**
Specialist Skills:	**Hiding his victims' bodies.**

Horrible Deeds: Gangland and contract killings.

Lucky Luciano earned his nickname by winning at gambling and avoiding arrest. By the age of twenty-nine he was second in command to Joe Masseria, a powerful New York gangland boss. In 1929 he was abducted by four rival gangsters, stabbed with an ice pick, had his throat slit from ear to ear and was left for dead on a beach – but he survived. Two years later he assassinated his boss, Masseria. To make sure of his position of power, he also gunned down a rival gangland boss, Salvatore Maranzano.

Luciano became the most powerful gangster in the whole of America and formed a group of contract killers known as Murder Incorporated, who were responsible for 1,000 deaths in their first year of business alone. The killers were good at making sure that bodies were never found, often encasing them in concrete before throwing them in the river. Luciano was finally arrested and imprisoned in 1936 but, because he proved useful to the government, his sentence was changed and he was allowed to go and spend the rest of his life in Italy.

Answer: b

Piero Manzoni

Nationality: Italian
Born: 1934
Died: 1963
Occupation: Artist

Horrible Deed: Canning his own poo.

Manzoni's artwork includes ninety cans of his own poo. Since he created them, many of the cans have exploded, probably due to expanding gases. In 2002, the Tate in London paid £22,300 for one of Manzoni's cans.

C Manoharan

Aka:	**Snake Manu**
Nationality:	**Indian**
Born:	**1978**

Horrible Deeds: Eating worms and putting snakes up his nose.

Snake Manu is a record-breaking eater of earthworms: in 2003 he swallowed 200 worms, each measuring at least ten centimetres, in thirty seconds. He also feeds live grass snakes into his mouth and out through his nose, which he describes as "snake flossing", and claims to have done the same with cobras and other poisonous snakes. Snake Manu discovered his nasal abilities when he was eight, when he would amuse his classmates by sticking erasers and other objects up his nose and bringing them out through his mouth.

Queen Marguerite de Valois

Nationality:	**French**
Born:	**1553**
Died:	**1615**
Occupation:	**Queen of Navarre (1572-1589) and of France (1589-1610)**

Horrible Deeds: Keeping a collection of embalmed hearts.

Despite being married to Henry IV, Marguerite had lots of boyfriends. She is supposed to have had the hearts of any dead boyfriends embalmed and sealed in separate boxes, which she carried in the pockets of her skirt at all times. Marguerite narrowly escaped being murdered on her wedding night on the orders of her brother, *Charles IX*.

Mary I

Aka:	**Bloody Mary**
Nationality:	**English**
Born:	**1516**
Died:	**1558**
Occupation:	**Queen of England (1553-1558)**

Horrible Deeds: Executing hundreds of people by having them burned at the stake.

Anyone who wasn't a Catholic could be accused of heresy, and Mary made sure that anyone found guilty would suffer the horrible punishment of being burned alive. Mary had 300 people burned at the stake in the five years of her reign.

John Dudley, Duke of Northumberland, was in charge of a plot to make Lady Jane Grey queen instead of Mary, so Mary had him executed in a particularly horrible way. Lady Jane Grey was only fifteen years old but Mary showed no mercy and had her beheaded. Sir Thomas Wyatt led another plot against Mary in 1554: he was executed and his head hung from a gallows in Hyde Park, while the rest of his body was divided and displayed on gibbets around the city. Anyone else Mary suspected of being a rebel was dealt with in the same way.

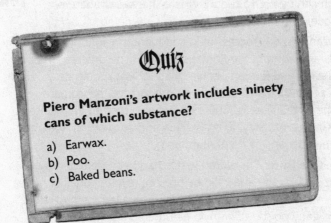

Quiz

Piero Manzoni's artwork includes ninety cans of which substance?

a) Earwax.
b) Poo.
c) Baked beans.

Mithradates VI

Aka:	**Mithradates the Great**
Nationality:	**Pontic (Pontus is now in Turkey)**
Born:	**About 132 BC**
Died:	**63 BC**
Occupation:	**King of Pontus (120-63BC)**
Specialist Skills:	**Fighting the Romans; being ruthless**

Horrible Deeds: Imprisoning and possibly murdering his mother; massacring people.

Mithradates was a child when he became king, so his mother ruled for him. He was always suspicious that she would poison him, so Mithradates took small doses of

M

poison to make himself immune. Eventually he had his mother thrown into prison, where she was probably murdered on his orders.

Mithradates was successful in conquering neighbouring lands and fighting the Romans. In 88 BC he ordered that all the Italian and Roman people living in Asia should be massacred so that there was no support for the Romans – maybe as many as 80,000 died. He also tried to intimidate the Greeks into staying on his side and against the Romans by having many of them murdered.

Horrible End: After Mithradates had been defeated by *Pompey*, his own army, led by his son, revolted against him. Mithradates tried to poison himself but failed (perhaps due to his early poison-taking) so he ordered a soldier to kill him. His body was sent to Pompey.

Sir Thomas More

Nationality:	**English**
Born:	**1477**
Died:	**1535**
Occupation:	**Lord Chancellor of England (1529 - 1532)**

Horrible Deed: See Horrible End.

Horrible End: Sir Thomas was beheaded in 1535 because he wouldn't acknowledge Henry VIII as Head of the Church. More's head was then boiled and displayed on a pole on London Bridge. Thomas More's daughter, Margaret Roper, managed to retrieve the head by bribing the bridge-keeper.

She took it home and preserved it in spices. After Margaret's death in 1544, she and her father's head were buried together.

al-Mu'tadid

Nationality:	**Moorish**
Born:	**?**
Died:	**AD 902**
Occupation:	**Caliph of Spain (892 - 902)**

Horrible Deed: Decorating the terraces of his Alcazar palace in Seville with the skulls of his decapitated enemies.

Horrible End: al-Mu'tadid is thought to have been poisoned by his political rivals.

Jack Mytton

Nationality:	**English**
Born:	**1796**
Died:	**1834**
Occupation:	**Aristocrat and daredevil**

Horrible Deeds: Various daring but horrible acts.

Mytton once set himself on fire to cure himself of the hiccups, and was badly burned as a result. He kept a bear, which he rode at one of his dinner parties – the bear bit and ate part of his leg but Mytton seemed unconcerned. He would sometimes rob guests who were on the way home from his parties, and he once purposely overturned a carriage because his companion said he'd never been in a crash.

Horrible End: Mytton was a very heavy drinker and died of alcohol poisoning.

Quiz

Which Roman emperor tried several times to kill his own mother?

a) Caligula
b) Nero
c) Augustus

 Nero

Aka: **Nero Claudius Caesar Augustus Germanicus**

Nationality: **Ancient Roman**

Born: **AD 37**

Died: **AD 68**

Occupation: **Emperor of Rome (AD 54-68)**

Horrible Deeds: Executing people, including his own mother and (probably) two wives.

Nero tried to kill his mother *Agrippina* on various occasions: several times with poison, once by trying to collapse a ceiling on top of her bed, and once by sinking a boat in the Bay of Naples (she managed to swim ashore). In AD 59 he succeeded, probably by sending an assassin to club her to death.

N

In AD 62 Nero accused his wife Octavia of having other boyfriends and had her executed, because he wanted to marry someone else. His new wife, Poppaea Sabina, was killed too – one report says that Nero kicked her to death for complaining that he'd come home late.

Nero was suspected of setting fire to Rome, which probably wasn't true. But he did take advantage of it by building himself a huge golden palace on the large area destroyed by the fire. He blamed the Christians for starting the fire, and so had many of them arrested and crucified, burned, or thrown to wild animals in the games.

After a plot against him was discovered in AD 65, Nero began executing politicians, generals and any other important Romans who'd made him suspicious. Eventually there was a rebellion against him and Galba was made emperor. Nero was sentenced to be flogged to death.

Horrible End: Rather than face his sentence, Nero committed suicide by stabbing himself with a dagger.

Paul Oldfield

Aka: **Mr Methane**

Nationality: **English**

Born: **1966**

Occupation: **Entertainer.**

Horrible Deeds: Making a living from farting.

Paul Oldfield calls what he does "Controlled Anal Voicing". His Mr Methane act includes farting tunes (both classical and modern), blowing out candles and farting a dart to burst a balloon. He is currently the world's only full-time performing "flatulist". (See also *Joseph Pujol*.)

Opechancanough

Nationality:	**Native American**
Born:	**About 1545**
Died:	**1644**
Occupation:	**Chief of the Powhatan Indians**

Horrible Deeds: Killing more than 800 English settlers.

The English and the Indian people had been living together peacefully in Virginia, but Opechancanough became angry because the English settlers were taking more and more land. In 1622 he attacked the settlement and killed 347 people. Twelve years later Opechancanough led another attack and this time he killed about five hundred, but he was captured.

Horrible End: Opechancanough was murdered while in custody, probably by a prison guard.

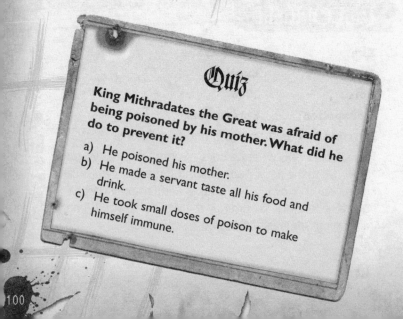

Quiz

King Mithradates the Great was afraid of being poisoned by his mother. What did he do to prevent it?

a) He poisoned his mother.

b) He made a servant taste all his food and drink.

c) He took small doses of poison to make himself immune.

John Michael Osbourne

Aka: Ozzy Osbourne

Nationality: English

Born: 1948

Occupation: Singer and celebrity

Horrible Deeds: Biting the heads of animals and defiling a historic monument.

As part of his stage act in 1981, Ozzy would throw raw meat at the audience and audience members would respond by throwing back dead animals. At a concert in Iowa, USA, someone threw a live bat on stage and Ozzy bit its head off (he claimed he thought it was a toy bat). Later, at a meeting with his record label, Ozzy planned to release two doves into the air, but instead released one dove and bit the head off the other.

Ozzy was once imprisoned for peeing on the historic Alamo building in Texas while drunk.

Answer: b

P

William Palmer

Aka:	**The Rugeley Poisoner**
Nationality:	**English**
Born:	**1824**
Died:	**1856**
Occupation:	**Doctor and murderer**

Horrible Deeds: Murdering maybe as many as fourteen people.

William Palmer was fond of gambling and got himself into a lot of debt. Over the years several people close to him had died: his mother, leaving him property, his wife, who had recently been insured for £13,000, and a gambling friend to whom Palmer owed money. While he was drinking at a racecourse bar, Palmer's friend, Alfred Cook, collapsed. Palmer helpfully went to collect his friend's winnings, and

looked after him for the next few days. Cook died a few days later, but his father became suspicious. When doctors looked at the body they discovered that Cook had been poisoned. Palmer was arrested and found guilty of the murder, but it's thought he might have poisoned thirteen other people, including his wife and mother.

Horrible End: Palmer was hanged at Stafford prison.

Mike Patton

Nationality: American
Born: 1968
Occupation: Singer

Horrible Deed: While Mike Patton was performing with his band Faith No More, a member of the audience peed into a bottle and threw it on stage. Then Patton did something even more disgusting by opening the bottle and pouring the contents over his head.

Peter I

Aka: Peter the Great
Nationality: Russian
Born: 1672
Died: 1725
Occupation: Tsar of Russia (1682-1725)

Horrible Deeds: Killing thousands of workers and sentencing his son to death.

St Petersburg was built on Peter the Great's orders. Tens of thousands of workers were needed to construct the city, and they were treated appallingly: they were underfed, had to live in cramped and filthy conditions, and were punished with whipping, mutilation and execution. Many starved or died of disease. At least 30,000 workers were killed in the building of St Petersburg, which is still known as "the city built on bones".

While his workers were suffering, Peter formed a drinking club he called "The All-Drunken Synod of Fools and Jesters", who met up to get drunk and eat strange food including foxes, cats and rats. Peter was also notorious for performing tooth extractions on his friends.

Peter was suspicious that his son and heir to the throne, Alexis, was plotting against him. Alexis was tortured and sentenced to death, but died in prison before he could be officially executed.

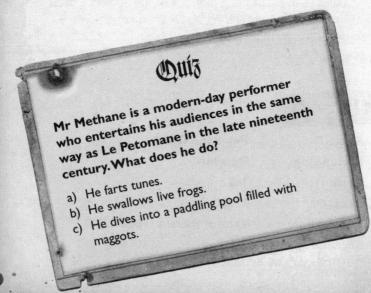

Quiz

Mr Methane is a modern-day performer who entertains his audiences in the same way as Le Petomane in the late nineteenth century. What does he do?

a) He farts tunes.
b) He swallows live frogs.
c) He dives into a paddling pool filled with maggots.

Philip I

Aka:	**Philip the Handsome**
Nationality:	**Belgian**
Born:	**1478**
Died:	**1506**
Occupation:	**King of Castile (briefly, in 1506)**

Horrible Deed: Accompanying his wife around Spain after his own death.

Horrible End: Philip died of a fever, possibly killed by one of his wife's love potions, but stayed close to her side: *Juana the Mad* refused to bury his coffin but kept it with her, checking on the body every so often.

Francisco Pizarro

Nationality:	**Spanish**
Born:	**About 1475**
Died:	**1541**
Occupation:	**Conquistador**
Specialist Skills:	**Conquering and getting rich.**

Horrible Deeds: Killing Incas.

During Pizarro's first expedition to South America he discovered that the wealthy Incan Empire existed in the area now known as Peru. In 1531 he left Spain for Peru for a second time, with about 200 soldiers and 60 horses. Pizarro asked for a meeting with the emperor of the Incas, Atahualpa, who had an army of 30,000 men. When

Answer: a

Atahualpa arrived at Pizarro's camp with a bodyguard of a few thousand lightly armed men, Pizarro's soldiers attacked, using firearms and crossbows, and soon defeated the emperor and his men. Most of the Incas were killed. Pizarro held Atahualpa to ransom, but despite the fact that he paid Pizarro by filling his prison cell with fabulous gold and silver, Atahualpa was executed by strangulation. Pizarro seized the whole of Peru and divided its wealth between himself and fellow Spaniards.

Horrible End: Pizarro was killed by a Spanish enemy – it's said he died a slow death, drawing a cross on the ground in his own blood and kissing it before he died.

Pompey

Aka:	Gnaeus Pompeius Magnus, Pompey the Great, The Teenage Butcher
Nationality:	Ancient Roman
Born:	106 BC
Died:	48 BC
Occupation:	General and politician

Horrible Deeds: Pompey was known as "The Teenage Butcher" for his ruthlessness in battle when he was a young man – he led successful campaigns, wiped out pirates and killed thousands of escaping rebels from the *Spartacus* slave rebellion. He supported *Sulla* and his proscriptions, but finally fell out with his old friend *Julius Caesar* and fled to Egypt.

Horrible End: Pompey was murdered when he got to

Egypt. His head was cut off and presented to Caesar in a
basket.

Bartolomeo Prignano

Aka: **The Mad Pope, Pope Urban VI**
Nationality: **Italian**
Born: **About 1318**
Died: **1389**
Occupation: **Pope (1378-1389)**

Horrible Deeds: Torturing and executing his cardinals.

When Bartolomeo was made Pope he started as he meant
to go on: he got drunk at the feast, started a row and
assaulted one of his cardinals. Later, he had six of his
cardinals horribly tortured and all but one of them killed –
either by burying them alive or putting them into sacks and
drowning them in the sea.

Horrible End: People strongly suspected that the Mad
Pope had been poisoned by one of his many enemies.

Joseph Pujol

Aka: **Le Petomane**
Nationality: **French**
Born: **1857**
Died: **1945**
Occupation: **Entertainer.**

Horrible Deeds: Making a living from farting.

Answer: c

Joseph Pujol was the highest paid entertainer of his day when he appeared in Paris as Le Petomane (in English "The Fart Maniac") at the end of the nineteenth century. Joseph's act involved playing tunes and blowing out candles (like his modern successor, *Paul Oldfield*).

Quiz

Which singer was put in prison for peeing on a historic building?

a) Ozzy Osbourne
b) Mick Jagger
c) Britney Spears

Marc Quinn

Nationality: English

Born: 1964

Occupation: Artist

Horrible Deeds: Creating a sculpture of his head made out of his own blood.

Marc Quinn drew 4.5 litres of his own blood over a period of five months. He poured the blood into a mould he'd made of his head, and then froze it. The sculpture, called Self, was first exhibited in 1991. See also *Shihan Hussaini*.

Gilles de Rais

Nationality: French

Born: 1404

Died: 1440

Occupation: Baron

Horrible Deeds: Killing more than a 100 children.

Gilles de Rais was a wealthy man with a good reputation, but his career ended with a famous trial. He was accused of having tortured and murdered more than 140 children. He confessed to the crimes after he was threatened with torture.

Horrible End: Baron de Rais was hanged in 1440.

Sir Walter Raleigh

Nationality: English

Born: About 1554

Died: 1618

Occupation: Soldier and explorer

Specialist Skills: Writing poetry and a "History of the World"

Horrible Deeds: See Horrible End.

Horrible End: Sir Walter was accused of treason by James I and executed in 1618. His severed head was kept by his wife *Elizabeth Throgmorton* in a leather bag until she died, and afterwards Raleigh's son Carew looked after it until his death in 1666. Carew was buried in his father's tomb with the head, but fourteen years later Carew's body was dug up and reburied, with the head of Sir Walter, in West Horsley, Surrey.

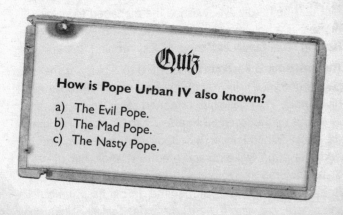

Quiz

How is Pope Urban IV also known?

a) The Evil Pope.
b) The Mad Pope.
c) The Nasty Pope.

R

Gregori Rasputin

Aka:	**The Mad Monk, Grigory Yefimovich Novykh**
Nationality:	**Russian**
Born:	**About 1872**
Died:	**1916**
Occupation:	**Monk**

Horrible Deeds: Being drunk, disorderly and smelly, and meeting with a horrible end.

Rasputin's family name was Novykh but Gregori was known as Rasputin (Russian for "debauched one") from an early age because he had lots of girlfriends and spent most of his time getting drunk and behaving badly. He said he believed it was impossible to be properly forgiven by God until you'd sinned properly – which gave him an excuse to do a lot of sinning. A police report from 1915 says he was caught exposing himself in a restaurant. Despite all this, and the fact that he hardly ever washed, he managed to style himself as a holy man and ended up best friends with the Russian royal family and more or less running Russia.

Horrible End: Rasputin was invited to a party at the palace of Prince Felix Yussoupov by a group who planned his murder. They gave him poisoned cakes and poisoned wine but neither seemed to affect him, so they shot him in the chest. When Prince Yussoupov went to inspect the body, Rasputin woke up and tried to strangle him. Yussoupov ran away in terror. The assassins returned to finish the job and, after some time, found Rasputin outside the palace, crawling towards the gate. They shot him again and gave him a beating, then tied him up and threw him into the freezing River Neva. Finally he died.

Francois Ravaillac

Nationality: French

Born: 1578

Died: 1610

Occupation: Teacher and lawyer

Horrible Deed: Stabbed Henry VI of France to death in 1610.

Horrible End: Francois Ravaillac had to face the same horrific punishment as Robert Damiens: he was tortured and then torn apart by attaching his limbs to horses and driving them in different directions.

Richard I

Aka: Richard the Lionheart

Nationality: English

Born: 1157

Died: 1199

Occupation: King of England (1189-1199)

Specialist Skills: Crusading

Horrible Deeds: Executing thousands of prisoners of war, and going to war against his own father.

R

Richard's father, Henry II, suggested that Richard might share part of his kingdom with his brother. Richard's response was to join forces with Henry's enemy, French King Philip II, and go to war against his father. Henry II died soon after. Richard went to fight in the Crusades and, after a victory at Acre, he executed 2,700 Muslim prisoners one by one, as a warning to the Muslim army.

Horrible End: Richard died of a gangrenous crossbow wound.

Richard III

Nationality:	**English**
Born:	**1452**
Died:	**1485**
Occupation:	**King of England (1483-1485) and wicked uncle**

Horrible Deed: Killing his nephews (probably).

When Edward IV, died, his successor was the twelve-year-old Edward V. Richard, Edward V's uncle, was made "Protector" because of the young king's age. But, instead of looking after his nephew, Richard got a bishop to declare that Edward's parents had never been properly married, which meant that Edward couldn't be king. Then he imprisoned Edward and his nine-year-old brother in the Tower of London. They were never seen again. It's very likely that Richard had them murdered. In the seventeenth century, work on a stairwell at the Tower revealed the skeletons of two young boys, aged about nine and twelve.

Horrible End: Two years after Richard became king, he was killed in battle and Henry Tudor took the crown.

Maximilien-François-Marie-Isidore de Robespierre

Nationality:	**French**
Born:	**1758**
Died:	**1794**
Occupation:	**Lawyer and French revolutionary**

Horrible Deeds: Sent thousands of people to the guillotine.

Robespierre became Head of the Committee of Public Safety after the French Revolution in 1793, which meant that anyone he chose could be sent to the guillotine. During his "Reign of Terror" he sent thousands to their deaths, including any of his fellow revolutionaries who wanted to stop the Terror. About 30,000 people were guillotined all together. Eventually, other revolutionaries who wanted to end the bloodbath had Robespierre arrested. He was sentenced to death by guillotine.

Horrible End: Robespierre tried to kill himself before being taken to the guillotine but only succeeded in damaging his his face. He was guillotined before cheering crowds. 108 of his supporters were also killed.

Ezzelino da Romano

Aka:	**Son of the Devil**
Nationality:	**Italian**
Born:	**1194**
Died:	**1259**
Occupation:	**Evil tyrant**

Horrible Deeds: Torturing and murdering people.

Ezzelino spent over twenty years terrorising northern Italy. He ordered several massacres: at Friola, all the inhabitants of the town were horribly mutilated and left to die; when he defeated Brescia, hundreds were burned alive or tortured to death; at Padua, about 5,000 people (a quarter of the population) were murdered.

Horrible End: Ezzelino was captured in battle and imprisoned. He killed himself by ripping the bandages from his wounds and bleeding to death.

Quiz

How was Walter Raleigh remembered by his wife after his execution?

a) She kept a lock of his blood-stained hair.
b) She had his body buried in her garden.
c) She kept his head in a leather bag.

R.I.P.

R

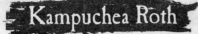

Kampuchea Roth

Nationality: Cambodian
Born: 1922
Occupation: Guru (spiritual leader)

Horrible Deed: Not washing for more than 60 years. Roth says his devotion to Buddhism prevents him from letting water touch his skin or long, matted dreadlocks.

Answer: c

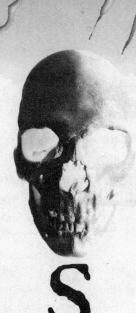

S

Sado

Nationality:	**Korean**
Born:	**1735**
Died:	**1762**
Occupation:	**Crown Prince of Korea**

Horrible Deeds: Murdering his servants.

Sado began to have delusions and became afraid of the sky and particular written words. After his mother died, he got worse and became violent towards his servants and officials, killing several of them. He murdered one official and stuck the man's head on a stick, which he showed to the women of the court. He explained, "It relieves my pent-up anger to kill people or animals when I am feeling depressed or on edge".

Horrible End: On the orders of his father, King Yongjo,

Sado was put inside a locked wooden chest and left to die. Sado's servants were also put to death.

Santorio Sanctorius

Nationality: Italian
Born: 1561
Died: 1636
Occupation: Doctor

Horrible Deed: Weighing his own excrement.

Santorio Sanctorius made a large set of scales and carefully weighed himself, everything he ate and everthing that came out of either end. After 30 years of experiments, Santorio found that what went in weighed more than what came out.

Nadir Shah

Nationality: Persian
Born: 1688
Died: 1747
Occupation: Emperor of Persia (1736-1747)
Specialist Skills: Conquering; frightening people.

Horrible Deeds: Blinding his son and torturing and killing many other people.

Having amassed a huge empire, Nadir Shah began to show signs of madness. He accused his son, Reza Quili Mira, of plotting to kill him and had him blinded. Then he ordered the execution of everyone who had witnessed the blinding. He began having people tortured and executed wherever he went: towers were built of the severed heads of those he'd had killed on one journey in 1747.

Horrible End: Nadir Shah was attacked and beheaded by two of his own commanders while he was asleep.

Shaka

Nationality:	**Zulu**
Born:	**About 1787**
Died:	**1828**
Occupation:	**Zulu King (1816-1828)**
Specialist Skill:	**Conquering.**

Horrible Deeds: Ordering amass executions.

Shaka's army conquered most of southeast Africa and Natal, killing maybe as many as two million people on the way. He became increasingly cruel to his own people. After Shaka's mother died in 1827, he ordered the execution of about 7,000 Zulus. For a year afterwards, no crops were planted and no milk could be used, so that the people were half-starved. Shaka even ordered thousands of cows to be killed , so that (he said) their calves would grieve for their mothers.

Horrible End: Shaka was hacked to death by his half-brothers, *Dingane* and Mhlangane. They threw his body into an empty grain pot and filled it with stones.

David Sherry

Nationality: **Northern Irish**

Born: **1974**

Occupation: **Artist**

Horrible Deed: David Sherry's performance artwork, Stitching, is a video of the artist sewing balsa wood soles onto his feet while he gives instructions on how to do it.

George Joseph Smith

Aka: **The Brides in the Bath Murderer**

Nationality: **English**

Born: **1872**

Died: **1915**

Occupation: **Swindler**

Horrible Deeds: Marrying several different women at the same time and killing three of them.

Smith was legally married in 1898 but later married three other women (while still married to the first one) under a false name. He killed each of his three later wives by drowning them in the bath, claiming that they'd had fits. Each of them had money he stood to inherit. Smith's first wife, Beatrice, believed her husband to be an antiques dealer.

Horrible End: Smith was arrested for the murders, found guilty and hanged at Maidstone prison.

Lazzaro Spallanzani

Nationality:	**Italian**
Born:	**1729**
Died:	**1799**
Occupation:	**Priest and scientist.**
Specialist Skill:	**Having a strong stomach.**

Horrible Deed: Spallanzani experimented with his digestion process by eating his own vomit, throwing it up again, eating the vomited vomit, throwing that up and then eating the end result (which was vomited, vomited vomit).

Quiz

Who ended up with his right arm in Newcastle, his left arm in Berwick, his right leg in Perth, his left leg in Aberdeen and his head on a pole on London Bridge?

a) William Wallace.
b) Robert Bruce.
c) Rob Roy MacGregor.

Spartacus

Nationality:	**Thracian**
Born:	**About 109 BC**
Died:	**71 BC**
Occupation:	**Gladiator and leader of a slave revolt**

Horrible Deed: Spartacus escaped from gladiator school with a group of about 70 other gladiators, raised an army of 70,000 rebel slaves, and defeated two Roman legions. But they met with a horrible end.

Horrible End: Spartacus was killed in a final battle against the Romans led by *Crassus* – it's said that his body was cut into pieces and never found. Crassus had 6,000 rebel slaves crucified. *Pompey* captured and killed 5,000 more slaves who had escaped after the battle.

Jacob Sprenger

Nationality:	**German**
Born:	**About 1437**
Died:	**1494**
Occupation:	**Priest and Inquisitor Extraordinary**

Horrible Deeds: Responsible for the deaths of hundreds of "witches".

In his position as Inquisitor Extraordinary, Sprenger was expected to uncover witches and see that they were duly punished with execution. He was extremely successful – it's thought that he found as many as 500 victims. He also wrote the *Malleus Maleficarum*, or "The Hammer of

Witches", a sort of guidebook for witchhunters. In the book he says that gossip is enough evidence to bring a suspected witch to trial, and recommends torture, in particular the use of red hot irons.

Stevie Starr

(Aka:	**The Regurgitator)**
Nationality:	**Scottish**
Born:	**1963**
Occupation:	**Entertainer**

Horrible Deeds: Stevie Starr has the ability to swallow various household objects, and even live creatures, and bring them up again in any order (and still alive). He earned a world record in 1998 when he successfully regurgitated a billiard ball, a bumble bee and a goldfish.

Alexander Stewart

Aka:	**The Wolf of Badenoch**
Nationality:	**Scottish**
Born:	**? 1343**
Died:	**? 1405**
Occupation:	**Lord of Badenoch and Earl of Buchan**

Horrible Deeds: Burning and destroying homes, cathedrals and entire towns.

Alexander Stewart earned his nickname by ruling Badenoch

cruelly. Anyone who upset him would have his home burned down and might end up in his castle dungeon, which Stewart always kept flooded with freezing water.

The Wolf had deserted his wife and, in 1390, the Bishop of Moray reprimanded him and told him to go back to her. Stewart flew into a rage and burned down the Bishop's cathedral at Elgin, as well as the town of Forres and two monasteries.

Horrible End: According to legend, Alexander ended his days playing chess with the Devil himself at Ruthven Castle. When the Devil won, Alexander Stewart went up in smoke along with his castle.

Mary Stewart

Aka:	**Mary Queen of Scots**
Nationality:	**Scottish**
Born:	**1542**
Died:	**1587**
Occupation:	**Queen of Scotland (1542-67)**

Horrible Deeds: Killing a husband (probably) and having someone tried and beheaded when he was already dead.

Mary married her cousin, Henry Darnley. He took part in the brutal murder of Mary's secretary, Riccio, who was stabbed fifty-three times while Mary was forced to watch. Mary got a new boyfriend, James Hepburn the Earl of Bothwell. It's very likely that she planned the murder of Darnley with him, though it was never proved. Darnley was strangled trying to escape from his house, which had been blown up with gunpowder. Mary was out with the Earl of Bothwell at the time.

Mary had various people executed during her reign, but one of them was already dead. In 1562, the Earl of Huntly led a rebellion against Mary. Huntly's force was defeated and the Earl died on the battlefield. But Mary had his body preserved and brought back to Edinburgh so that it could stand trial for treason – he was found guilty (of course) and Mary attended his execution.

Horrible End: Mary was imprisoned in 1568 and beheaded eighteen years later on the orders of her cousin, *Elizabeth I* of England.

Walter Stewart

Nationality:	**Scottish**
Born:	**About 1360**
Died:	**1437**
Occupation:	**Earl of Atholl and Caithness**

Horrible Deed: Assassinated King James I of Scotland.

Walter Stewart was King James I's uncle, but that didn't stop him being part of the group who assassinated the king in 1437. Along with *Sir Robert Graham*, the Earl of Atholl was caught soon after the murder.

Horrible End: Stewart's execution lasted three days. First he had his legs pulled out of their sockets, then a red-hot crown was put on his head. He was then dragged through the streets of Edinburgh. Finally he was hanged, drawn and quartered.

Sulla

(aka Lucius Cornelius Sulla)

Nationality:	**Ancient Roman**
Born:	**138 BC**
Died:	**78 BC**
Occupation:	**Dictator of the Roman Republic (82-79 BC)**

Horrible Deeds: Killing hundreds in his "proscriptions".

Sulla won Rome's first civil war and became sole ruler of Rome. One of his first acts was to draw up a list of men he wanted dead – the list, or "proscription", was put on public display. All the people on the list were treated as outlaws, which meant that anyone had the right to kill them, their children were banned from become politicians, and all of their property was confiscated and sold off cheaply – this was how *Crassus* came by a lot of his wealth. Forty senators (high-ranking politicians) were on Sulla's lists, as well as 1,600 wealthy citizens. Few of them escaped death. Sulla also ordered the execution of about 3,000 prisoners who'd fought against him in the civil war.

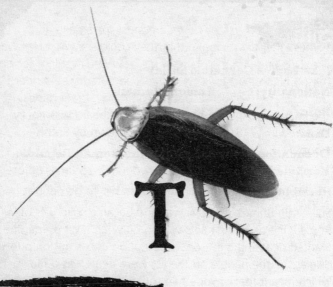

Edward Teach

Aka:	**Blackbeard**
Nationality:	**English**
Born:	**1680**
Died:	**1718**
Occupation:	**Pirate**
Specialist Skills:	**Plundering; being criminally insane**

Horrible Deeds: Robbing, killing and random acts of cruelty.

Blackbeard began his career in piracy in 1713, attacking and robbing ships in the Caribbean. He became famous for his hellish appearance – he had an extravagant black beard, stuck lighted matches under his hat, and carried six pistols. He once set fire to various objects below decks and then forced his crew to stay down amongst the smoke and flames – he said it was so that they could see what Hell was like. Drinking wth members of his crew one evening, for no reason Blackbeard took two pistols and fired them under the table: he shot his second-in-command, Israel Hands, in the kneecap, crippling him for life. Blackbeard was finally captured in 1718, when he was shot down by British troops.

Horrible End: Blackbeard was wounded 25 times before he finally died. Lieutenant Maynard, leading the British troops, cut off Blackbeard's head and stuck it on the prow of his ship. The other members of Blackbeard's crew were hanged except for two – including Israel Hands.

Quiz

How did George Joseph Smith kill three of his wives?

a) By strangling them with his tie.
b) By smothering them with a pillow.
c) By drowning them in the bath.

T

Theodoric

Aka: Theodoric the Great

Nationality: Ostrogoth

Born: About AD 454

Died: AD 526

Occupation: King of the Ostrogoths (ruled from 471) and King of Italy (493-526)

Specialist Skills: Conquering.

Horrible Deeds: Murdering his co-ruler and his family and supporters.

Theodoric agreed to share power with Odoacer, who was ruler of Italy. Then he invited Odoacer to a banquet, where he murdered him, his son and his chief ministers. Theodoric then killed Odoacer's wife and went on a ruthless hunt throughout Italy, killing any of Odoacer's supporters that he found. Theodoric also killed the top Roman politician Boethius - he accused him of treason and had him put to death without trial.

Elizabeth Throgmorton

Born: About 1570

Died: About 1647

Occupation: Lady-in-Waiting to Elizabeth I

Horrible Deeds: Keeping her dead husband's head in a bag.

Elizabeth was married to *Sir Walter Raleigh*, who was

beheaded in 1618. Sir Walter's body was buried, but
Elizabeth decided to keep his embalmed head in a red
leather bag, by her side, for the remaining 29 years of her
life.

Tiberius

Aka:	**Tiberius Caesar Augustus**
Nationality:	**Ancient Roman**
Born:	**42 BC**
Died:	**AD 37**
Occupation:	**Roman Emperor (AD 14-37)**

Horrible Deeds: Torturing and killing.

Tiberius spent his last years on the island of Capri. He built
himself several luxurious villas, complete with torture
chambers where he enjoyed watching his victims suffer.
Towards the end of his life, many politicians and wealthy
Romans were accused of murdering Tiberius's son, Drusus,
or of plotting against Tiberius. He had so many important
Romans killed that most of his potential successors were
dead – he named his grand-nephew *Caligula* and grandson
Gemellus as his successors in his will.

Horrible End: Tiberius was old and sick for a long time,
and it's thought that Caligula or one of his supporters
might have suffocated him.

T

Timur

Aka:	**Timur the Lame, Tamerlane**
Nationality:	**Transoxanian (now Uzbekistan)**
Born:	**1336**
Died:	**1405**
Occupation:	**Nomadic ruler**
Specialist Skills:	**Conquering, plundering and pillaging**

Horrible Deeds: Leaving a trail of destruction across his huge empire.

Timur and his brother-in-law, Amir Husayn, defeated the ruler of Transoxania around 1366. Three years later, Timur had Amir Husayn assassinated and set out to restore the Mongol Empire of Genghis Khan.

Timur led his army across Persia, India and Russia, becoming famous for his cruelty as he went. While he occupied Moscow, revolts broke out in Persia but Timur made sure that they were stopped: cities were destroyed and the people killed, their skulls made into towers.

In 1398 Timur invaded India and left the city of Delhi in ruins and the 80,000 people who lived there dead. Three years later, Baghdad was also destroyed and another 20,000 people massacred.

Tomás de Torquemada

Nationality:	**Spanish**
Born:	**1420**

| Died: | 1498 |
| Occupation: | **Monk and Grand Inquisitor** |

Horrible Deeds: Torturing and executing people.

Torquemada reorganised the Spanish Inquisition, set up in 1478 by *King Ferdinand* and *Queen Isabella*, making it much more efficient (and bloodthirsty). He used torture to get people to confess to having beliefs that were opposed to the Church, using red-hot pincers, thumbscrews, stretching with weights and pulleys, and water torture. Once the prisoners had confessed, they were paraded through town, pelted with rubbish on the way, before having their crimes read out and receiving their sentence. Some prisoners might be whipped but most were handed over to the town officials to be burned at the stake. It's thought that about 2,000 prisoners were burned while Torquemada was in charge of the Inquisition.

Marie Tussaud

Nationality:	**French**
Born:	**1761**
Died:	**1850**
Occupation:	**Wax modeller and museum curator**

Horrible Deeds: Making death masks from guillotined heads.

During the French Revolution when thousands of people were executed, Madame Tussaud had the gruesome job of making death masks of the people who'd had their heads chopped off by the guillotine. She took the heads fresh

T

from the guillotine basket and made moulds from them to create wax masks. Some of the masks she made were for people who'd been Madame Tussaud's friends.

Marie Tussaud took her collection of death masks on a tour around Britain for the next 33 years. Finally she stopped touring and set up the famous Madame Tussaud's wax museum in London.

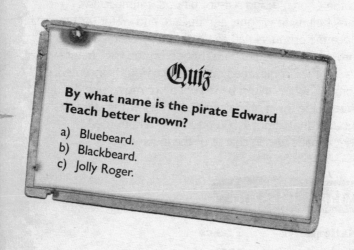

Quiz

By what name is the pirate Edward Teach better known?

a) Bluebeard.
b) Blackbeard.
c) Jolly Roger.

V

Vercingetorix

Nationality:	**Gaulish (Gaul is now part of France)**
Born:	**?**
Died:	**46 BC**
Occupation:	**Leader of the Gauls.**

Horrible Deeds: Vercingetorix held a meeting of tribes to unite them against the Romans; when one of the tribal chiefs argued with him, Vercingetorix had his ears cut off and one of his eyes gouged out.

Horrible End: Once Julius Caesar captured Vercingetorix, he was taken to Rome in chains and paraded in Caesar's triumphal procession in 52 BC. He was publicly beheaded six years later.

Answer: b

V

Giovanni da Verrazzano

Nationality: **Italian**
Born: **1485**
Died: **1528**
Occupation: **Explorer**

Horrible Deed: see Horrible End.

Horrible End: Giovanni da Verranzzano was exploring Florida, the Bahamas and the Lesser Antilles islands and rowed ashore in a small boat to meet the native inhabitants of the island of Guadaloupe. He soon discovered that the people were not friendly: they killed Giovanni and quickly cooked and ate him.

Andreas Vesalius

Nationality: **Belgian**
Born: **1514**
Died: **1564**
Occupation: **Doctor and anatomist**

Horrible Deeds: Body-snatching.

Like *John Hunter*, Vesalius was interested in human anatomy but couldn't find bodies to dissect – and in fact dissection was against the law in Belgium when he worked there. So Vesalius dug up corpses from graves, stole the bodies of criminals on public display or swiped them at the end of executions. Then he would hide the bodies in his room and dissect them there, keeping his gory work a secret.

Things became a lot easier when Vesalius moved to Padua in Italy – dissection wasn't banned there and a Paduan judge became interested in his work and kept him supplied with executed criminals.

Horrible End: Vesalius died in a shipwreck. The story goes that he was running away after he'd discovered that one of the bodies he was dissecting was still alive … but it's probably not true.

Gian Galeazzo Visconti

Nationality:	**Italian**
Born:	**1351**
Died:	**1402**
Occupation:	**Duke of Milan (1378-1402)**

Horrible Deeds: Torturing, killing and (probably) poisoning his brother.

Gian Galeazzo started off as joint ruler of Milan with his brother, Bernabò. When they came to power, one of the first things the brothers did was to hold a 40-day-long torture marathon: their unfortunate victims suffered amputations, eye-gougings and many other horrible tortures.

After a few years, Gian Galeazzo became suspicious that Bernabò wanted to take power for himself. In 1385 he captured his brother and imprisoned him – Bernabò died the same year, probably poisoned on Gian Galeazzo's orders.

Horrible End: Visconti died suddenly of the plague before he could continue his plans to take control of the whole of northern Italy.

V

Vitellius

Aka:	**Aulus Vitellius**
Nationality:	**Ancient Roman**
Born:	**AD 15**
Died:	**AD 69**
Occupation:	**Roman Emperor (in AD 69)**

Horrible Deeds: Vitellius had a reputation for excess and laziness and was known as "The Glutton". He met with a horrible end.

Horrible End: Vitellius was proclaimed emperor when Nero died, but when he arrived in Rome with his troops he found that Vespasian had also been proclaimed emperor. He failed to defeat Vespasian's troops and Vitellius was murdered by his own soldiers: he was tortured, killed and thrown into the River Tiber.

William I

Aka:	**William the Conqueror**
Nationality:	**French**
Born:	**About 1028**
Died:	**1087**
Occupation:	**King of England (1066-1087)**

Horrible Deed: When there was a rebellion in the north of England, William ordered that all homes, belongings and farm animals should be destroyed. As a result, thousands of innocent people died of starvation.

Horrible End: When William died, his body was too big for the stone tomb that had been made for him and had to be forced in. His corpse smelled so bad that the priests had to rush through the funeral service.

William Wallace

Aka:	**Braveheart, The Patriot**
Nationality:	**Scottish**
Born:	**About 1270**
Died:	**1305**
Occupation:	**Guardian of Scotland (1297-98)**

Horrible Deed: Skinning an enemy.

In 1297 Wallace organised an army to fight the English and defeated them at Battle of Stirling Bridge. After the battle Wallace is supposed to have stripped the skin off the defeated English leader, Hugh Cressingham, and used it as a belt – though this might just be a story told by the English.

Horrible End: Wallace was arrested near Glasgow in 1305 and taken to London, where he was hanged, drawn and quartered. Bits of his body were sent off to be put on display in various different parts of England and Scotland: his right arm was displayed on Newcastle bridge, his left arm was sent to Berwick, his right leg to Perth and his left leg to Aberdeen. According to one story, Wallace's left leg ended up as part of one of the walls in Saint Machars Cathedral, Aberdeen. His head was stuck on a pole on London Bridge.

W

Jonathan Wild

Nationality:	English
Born:	1682
Died:	1725
Occupation:	Master criminal

Horrible Deeds: Making money out of stolen goods then turning the thieves over to the police.

Wild set himself up as an honest gentleman who had connections in London's criminal underworld: if a victim of theft went to him, he might be able to find their stolen property and return it, for a fee. In fact Wild was just as guilty of the crimes as the burglars and pickpockets he controlled – they got a better price for stolen goods by going to Wild instead of a pawnbroker or a fence, but Wild had control over them because he could easily turn them in to the police. The penalty for theft was usually death and Wild is thought to have sent at least 100 men to be executed by turning them in when they upset him or weren't profitable enough.

Horrible End: Wild was eventually caught. He was taken to Tyburn gallows in 1725, pelted with mud and stones on the way. His body was later dissected by a surgeon and ended up in the Hunterian museum (see *John Hunter*) – his skeleton is still there today.

XYZ

Xerxes

Nationality:	**Persian**
Born:	**519 BC**
Died:	**465 BC**
Occupation:	**King of Persia (486-465 BC)**

Horrible Deeds: Killing his bridge builders.

Xerxes spent years raising a 360,000-strong army with which he hoped to defeat Greece. He ordered a bridge to be built across the Hellespont, a narrow sea crossing, to transport his army. But the bridge was wrecked in a storm and Xerxes had the builders in charge of constructing the bridge to be beheaded. He also ordered the sea to be given 300 lashes for causing the storm.

Horrible End: Xerxes was murdered, possibly by his son, Ataxerxes, who succeeded him.

Wu Zeitan

Aka:	**Wu Hou**
Nationality:	**Chinese**
Born:	**AD 625**
Died:	**AD 705**
Occupation:	**Empress of China (ruled from 655 and as Emperor from 690 to 705)**

Horrible Deeds: Killing off rivals to the throne and exiling her own sons.

China's only female emperor killed anyone who stood in her way to the throne. She accused the Emperor's wife, Empress Wang, of killing her (Wu's) daughter – she was believed and Wang was executed. It's said she got rid of another two of Emperor Kao Tsung's wives by drowning them in a wine barrel. In 655 she became empress herself, and when her husband became seriously ill five years later, Wu ran the country for him. By this time, all her opponents had been exiled or killed, including the emperor's uncle and all his relatives. She created a secret police force to spy on her enemies and ruthlessly jailed or killed anyone who opposed her.

When her husband died in 683 Wu's son came to the throne – but because he had an ambitious wife, Wu kicked him off the throne and had him exiled. She made her second son emperor, but she was the one with the real power. In 690 she took the throne herself and ruled for the next 15 years.

If you've enjoyed this book, now read:

THE
DISGUSTING
DICTIONARY

Tracey Turner

An A to Z of rude and horrid words

Ordinary dictionaries are full of rude words, but they're hidden among thousands of boring words. The Disgusting Dictionary has nothing but fascinatingly foul and revolting words. Inside you'll discover:

- the posh word for picking your nose
- 85 ways to say 'vomit'
- whether you have a bat-in-a-cave
- how to say 'poo' in French and 'snot' in Urdu
- the meaning of humgruffin and jobbernowl

Warning: it may put you off your dinner!

Available from good bookshops.

ISBN 0 340 88399 5   £4.99